Pope John Paul II
THE THEOLOGY OF THE BODY

(HUMAN LOVE IN THE DIVINE PLAN)

A SIMPLIFIED VERSION

BY:
REV. MSGR. VINCENT M. WALSH, J.C.D.

From the Vatican, August 22, 2002

Dear Monsignor Walsh,

The Holy Father has asked me to thank you for the gift of your simplified version of his catecheses on the *Theology of the Body.* He is most appreciative of your efforts to bring his teachings to the attention of a wider audience.

His Holiness will remember your intentions in his prayers. He cordially imparts his Apostolic Blessing as a pledge of joy and peace in the Lord.

Sincerely yours in Christ,

Monsignor Pedro López Quintana
Assessor

Monsignor Vincent M. Walsh
Presentation B.V.M. Church
204 Haverford Road
Wynnewood, PA 19096

The Theology of the Body – Full Text

Pope John Paul II called "The Theology of the Body" his "working term" for the 129 talks which he gave at his Wednesday General Audiences between September 1979 and November 1984. He specifically directed these talks to an explanation of human love in God's plan.

These talks were originally printed in the English edition of "L'Osservatore Romano". This "Simplified Version" is based upon the full text of these 129 talks contained in the book: "The Theology of the Body" published by:

Pauline Books and Media
50 St. Pauls Avenue
Boston, MA 02130-3491

Church of Philadelphia – Key of David

Because Key of David Publications is located within the Archdiocese of Philadelphia, our name is taken from the Letter to the Church of Philadelphia. *"The holy one, the true, who holds the key of David, who opens and no one shall close, who closes and no one shall open."* (Rev.3:7)

DEDICATION

This book is dedicated to the wonderful parishioners of Presentation BVM Parish, Wynnewood, PA (Archdiocese of Philadelphia), who have been my spiritual family since June 1990.

A special thanks to my priestly classmate, Archbishop John P. Foley, President of the Pontifical Council for Social Communications, for his help in facilitating the publication of this book.

KEY OF DAVID PUBLICATIONS

The success of Monsignor Walsh's early books in the 1970's led to the formation of Key of David Publications. A full catalog of publications can be obtained by contacting:

KEY OF DAVID PUBLICATIONS

Key of David Publications
Post Office Box 153
Merion, PA 19066
610-896-1970
http:\www.libertynet.org/˜revival

Library of Congress Control #: Pending

ISBN: 0-943374-86-3

Printed in the U.S.A.

Thanks to Mrs. Eileen Hering for her time and expertise in typing this book.

TABLE OF CONTENTS

Part Two
Christ's Sermon on the Mount

Part Three
St. Paul's Teaching on the Human Body

TABLE OF CONTENTS (cont'd.)

Part Four
Ethical Norms for Modern Communications

Part Five
Christ's Teaching on the Resurrection of the Body

Part Six
Christ's Teaching on Virginity for the Sake of the Kingdom

TABLE OF CONTENTS (cont'd.)

Part Seven
The Crowning Text – Ephesians 5:21-33

TABLE OF CONTENTS (cont'd.)

Page

Part Eight
Important Texts From the Old Testament

Table of Contents (cont'd.)

Part Nine
Reflections on the Encyclical "Humanae Vitae"

EXPLAINING "A SIMPLIFIED VERSION"

Encountering the Pope's Thoughts

Pope John Paul II has a "world-class" intellect, and every reader should have the privilege of directly encountering the Pope's thinking. In his brilliance, however, the Pope writes in a style which is difficult for the average reader. Therefore, the goal of this "simplified version" is to allow the brilliance of his thoughts to be grasped by a wider audience.

All of the words, thoughts and reasoning processes in this book are the Pope's. Nothing has been "watered down". Therefore, the reader will see the beauty of his ideas and the clear flow of his reasoning.

Beginning the Task

In February 2000, I read the words of George Weigel in his biography of Pope John Paul II which stressed the urgent need for the Pope's books to be made available to a wider audience. He wrote, "A secondary literature capable of 'translating' John Paul's thoughts into more accessible categories and vocabulary is badly needed" (Page 343).

These words led to the publishing of the Pope's philosophical book, "Love and Responsibility – A Simplified Version". Because of the success enjoyed by this book (since its publication in May 2001), I undertook the larger task of writing "The Theology of the Body – A Simplified Version".

Using a Method

The method of this <u>Simplified Version</u> was very similar to the first. The key thoughts of every paragraph were put into simple sentences and then these individual sentences were put back into the shorter and simplified paragraph.

The Pope's Words and Thoughts

In this Simplified Version, the reader will be in direct contact with the Pope's own words. Nothing is added or changed. Only the writing style is simplified. Hopefully, the result will be an "easy-to-read" experience which discovers the truly great theological insights of Pope John Paul II.

The Titles and Headings

Each of the talks has been given a title and some headings. These were not part of the original talks but were added by Monsignor Walsh. The original talks had no titles attached to them

August 15, 2002

Part One
The Original Unity of Man and Woman
(In the Book of Genesis)

1. A CONFLICT SETS THE STAGE

Jesus' Conflict With the Pharisees

When Jesus spoke of marriage, in the gospels of Matthew and Mark, he used the expression "from the beginning". What does this word "beginning" mean and why did Christ refer to it?

Jesus used this phrase when the Pharisees asked him, "Is it lawful to divorce one's wife for any cause?" Jesus responded "Have you not read that He who made them <u>from the beginning</u> made them male and female and said 'For this reason a man shall leave his father and mother and be joined to his wife and the two shall become one flesh?' So they are no longer two but one flesh?" (Mt 19:4-6)

The Pharisees retorted, "Why then did Moses command one to give a certificate of divorce, and to put her away?" (19:7). Jesus responded, "For your hardness of heart Moses allowed you to divorce your wives, but <u>from the beginning</u> it was not so" (Mt.19:8) (cf also Mark 10:2-12).

Jesus' New Approach

By His response, Jesus did not accept the Pharisees' approach to the question of divorce. Instead, He introduced another approach to this problem, based upon words from the Book of Genesis which were familiar to both Jesus and the Pharisees.

Jesus also described what He meant by "in the beginning". He quoted Genesis, "In the beginning the Creator made them male and female." (1:27) and "Therefore a man leaves his mother and his father and cleaves to his wife and they become one flesh." (2:24). Jesus made these texts normative statements because He added, "So they are no longer two, but one flesh. Therefore what God has joined together, let no man put asunder." (Mt.19:6). This word "asunder" is decisive. In these words, Jesus establishes

1

Genesis 2:24 as the principle of the unity and indissolubility of marriage. It is the word of God, expressed in the most ancient revelation.

The Original Innocence of Male and Female

However, Christ's words do much more than merely confirm the original law of the Creator. By using the phrase "from the beginning", He asked the Pharisees, (and ourselves) to reflect on the way mankind was created, precisely as "male and female". This will help us to understand God's law on the unity and indissolubility of marriage.

Christ, in directing his questioners to Genesis 2:24 showed that He did not approve of Moses' permission to divorce. When Jesus asked them to examine the state of original innocence, He indicated that God's norm had not lost its original force, even though man had lost his original innocence. Christ's reply, decisive and unequivocal, has normative conclusions for a theology of the body. *September 5, 1979*

2. TRUTHS FROM CHAPTER ONE OF GENESIS

The Uniqueness of Man's Creation

Christ's words "in the beginning" refer to the early chapters of Genesis, particularly the first two chapters. In the first chapter, the creation of mankind as male and female is inserted into a seven-day creation cycle. Although man is created as part of the visible world, he is given orders to subdue and to have dominion over that visible world (1:28). Although man is linked to the visible world by his body, he is not made in the likeness of the other creatures but only in the likeness of God (1:26). Although the seven-day cycle has a precise and graduated procedure, man is not created in any natural succession. Instead, God deliberately halts the process before bringing Adam and Eve into existence, and ponders His decision to create them in His own image and likeness.

The Special Relationship to God

This first chapter has special theological importance, based on man's special relationship to God. "In the image of God He created him." (1:27). Man, then, cannot be reduced to the visible world, and although he is corporeal, he cannot be fully explained in corporeal categories. Genesis also says explicitly that this special truth applies to both sexes. "God created man in his image – male and female he created them" (1:27).

Totally Objective

This first chapter is totally objective, free from any trace of subjectivism, and defining objective facts. It highlights three realities. First, mankind is created as male and female. Second, he is made in the image of God. Third, he is to multiply and have dominion. This first chapter contains a powerful teaching regarding the philosophical questions of "being" and "existence" (metaphysics). (A similarly important text is God saying to Moses, "I am who am." Exodus C.3). Notwithstanding certain plastic expressions, the chapter defines mankind in the dimensions of being and of existence, (more of a metaphysical than a physical definition). Being created in God's image corresponds to the mystery that man himself is to procreate others. Procreating is necessarily connected with a creation that is contingent (that is, does not necessarily have to exist).

Chapter One also contains the aspect of value in the philosophical category of "good", which appears in nearly all the days of creation, and reaches its culmination after the creation of man. "God saw everything that he had made, and behold it was very good." (1:31)

A Solid Basis for Study

Chapter One establishes a solid basis for a metaphysic (the study of reality), and for an anthropology (the study of man). It also provides an ethic (the study of right norms), because "being and good are interchangeable". Needless to say, this chapter has special significance for a theology of the body. *September 12, 1979*

3. ORIGINAL INNOCENCE RUINED BY SIN

Surprisingly Subjective

This second chapter, linked to original innocence and the first fall, has a quite different character, surprising us with a profundity not found in the first chapter. This profundity is subjective and psychological and is the most ancient recording of man's self-knowledge, containing the first evidence of human conscience. The text, with its primitive mythical character, provides us "in a nutshell" with nearly all the elements used in contemporary studies of man. Although providing the subjective aspect of creation, the text totally corresponds to the objective reality of man described in the first chapter, that is, as created "in the image of God".

Two Separate Creations

When Christ replied to the Pharisees, He referred to the first chapter and the creation of man as "male and female". Only later did He quote from the second chapter, "That is why a man leaves his father and mother and clings to his wife, and the two of them become one body" (2:24). This sentence describes the unity and indissolubility of marriage and speaks clearly of two separate creations, of man (2:5-7) and of woman (2:18-23).

This second chapter uses the Hebrew word "Adam" for man. However, once woman is created, the chapter uses the Hebrew word ish for man and ishshah, (meaning "taken from man"), for woman. When Jesus spoke of man (ish) clinging to his wife (ishshah), He linked "the beginning" to man's primitive innocence and to his later original sin.

The Marital Relationship

Three verses in this chapter speak of the marital relationship. "The Lord God then built up into woman the rib that he had taken from the man." (V 22) "This one, at last, is bone of my bone and flesh of my flesh; she shall be called woman because she was taken out of man." (V23) "Therefore a man leaves his father and his mother and cleaves to his wife and they become one flesh." (V 24)

Original Innocence and Sin

Genesis then says, "And the man and his wife were both naked, and they were not ashamed." (2:25). These words lead quickly into the first fall of man and woman, which is linked to "the tree of good and evil" (mentioned already in 2:17).

4

The Line of Demarcation

The third chapter of Genesis describes an entirely new situation and gives a <u>line of demarcation</u> between two distinct situations. The first situation was of original innocence. It was outside of any sphere of "knowledge of good and evil" (before man transgressed the Creator's prohibition). The second situation, after disobedience, shows that man finds himself within the sphere of "knowledge of good and evil", the state of human sinfulness.

The description of events clearly differentiates these two original situations. An essential difference emerges between the state of original innocence (integral nature) and of sinfulness (fallen nature). These two distinct states have fundamental significance for the theology of man and theology of the body.

September 19, 1979

4. INNOCENCE, SINFULNESS AND REDEMPTION

Continuity Between Innocence and Sinfulness

By referring to "in the beginning," Christ asked us to go back beyond the boundary of sinfulness and consider the previous state of original innocence. This boundary (between innocence and sinfulness) is linked to the tree of knowledge of good and evil, which highlights the two aspects of man's inner self (innocence and sinfulness). Both good and evil are part of man's knowledge, conscience, choice and decisions. Although the tree of knowledge of good and evil contrasts these two very different states of innocence and hereditary sinfulness, Christ's words "in the beginning" reveal an essential continuity and link between them.

A Prehistory of Innocence

Every person participates in a state of sin which is part of "historical man." However, every person also has a "prehistory", that is, a state of original innocence. We cannot understand our present state of sinfulness without referring to our fundamental innocence. The sinful dimension of human existence has a relationship to our human innocence, because we were created in God's image.

5

This remains true for all human persons, not just the two persons described in Genesis. Historical man is rooted in this revealed prehistory. Historical sinfulness can be explained (both for soul and body) only in reference to original innocence. Our state of lost grace always contains a reference to that original grace.

The Promise of Redemption

Christ's words "in the beginning" do not refer merely to the lost horizon of human innocence, but also to the mystery of redemption. Man, male and female, received a promise of redemption when God spoke to the serpent, "I will put an enmity between you and the woman and between your offspring and hers; He will strike at your head" (Genesis 3:15). Because of this proto-gospel, man immediately began to live in God's redemption. Historical man has both a history of sinfulness and a history of salvation. Although mankind is closed by sinfulness, he is opened by Christ's redemption.

Christ Redeems Our Bodies

Paul writes "We ourselves, who have the first fruits of the Spirit, groan inwardly as we await for ... the redemption of our bodies" (Rom.8:23). Remembering this perspective helps us to understand the indissolubility of marriage, which Christ taught when He spoke of "in the beginning". Believing in a "redemption of the body" guarantees a continuity and unity with man's original innocence, even though that innocence has been lost.

Redemption as a Guide to Understanding

Corporeal man is perceived mainly by experiences, and any interpretation of revelation must refer to man's experiences. Although our present historical experience necessarily stops at the threshold of innocence, we can use these experiences of innocence as a means to interpret Christ's words "in the beginning." In doing this, we will be guided by Paul's words, "We who have the first fruits of the Spirit groan inwardly as we wait for ... the redemption of our bodies." All subsequent chapters must reflect this redemption. *September 26, 1979*

6

5. REALIZING HE IS ALONE – ORIGINAL SOLITUDE

Two Distinct Creations

God said, "It is not good that man (male) should be alone; I will make him a helper fit for him" (2:18). In the second chapter, the creation of man (2:7) is deliberately kept distinct from the creation of woman (2:21-22). This distinction helps us to understand man's original solitude.

Because Adam represents all mankind (Eve is not yet created.), original solitude does not just refer to a male, but to every person (male and female) and has two meanings. The first meaning is not caused by the lack of female companionship, but comes from the human condition. The second does come from the lack of female companionship.

Man is Alone

The first chapter of Genesis ignored this problem of man's solitude. The second chapter, however, concentrates our attention on the fact that "man is alone". This problem existed even before mankind is described as "male and female". God made three decisions. First, He gave man the task "to till the ground" (2:5). Secondly, He placed man in the Garden of Eden, introducing the state of original happiness. Finally, He said,, "I will make a helper for him." All three must be examined.

Naming the Animals

By being made to name all the animals (2:19), man becomes aware of his superiority. He is not on the same footing as any other living species. Once he has given names to all the animals, man becomes aware that he is alone before God. He is still searching for his own name and definition. "Being alone", (even in the middle of all living creation) has a negative meaning, showing what man "is not". However, his inability to identify himself in the visible world also has a positive meaning. Aristotle calls this "the proximate genus" (category).

Different Because He Names

Man, alone before God, expresses a first self-definition. As he gives a name to each animal, man affirms that he is different from every animal. Man realizes he has a cognitive power. This brings him out of his own being and reveals man to himself. He is different from other living beings. He is alone precisely because he is "different from the visible world".

By naming everything else, man asserts himself as "person" in the visible world. The whole process (of naming animals) reveals to man that he is a human person with specific subjectivity. In Aristotle's words, man is a "self-conscious being".

October 10, 1979

6. MAN: PARTNER IN A COVENANT

Man's First Moments of Choice

In these early chapters, Genesis has portrayed man as a person with a unique subjectivity. God adds to this description when He gives man a command concerning all the trees, and specifically the tree of knowledge of good and evil. Man now faces moments of choice, of self-determination and of free will. This completes Genesis' outline of man, a creature endowed with personal subjectivity.

We can see that the original solitude includes self-consciousness and self-determination. "Being alone" shows man's ability to comprehend. It also shows why God decided to "make a helper for man" (2:18). By understanding man's original solitude, we can correctly interpret this whole creation of man and his original covenant with God.

Partner in a Covenant

The first chapter says that man was made in the image of God. The second chapter shows that man is a subject in a covenant with God. He is a "partner of the Absolute", and must consciously choose between good and evil, life and death. This first order from God (not to eat from the tree of knowledge) asks man to submissively depend upon the Creator. Man as "alone," has a unique, exclusive and unrepeatable relationship with God. This fulfills the definition that man is made in God's image.

Alone Because of Consciousness

Although man participates in visible creation, he arrives at the conclusion that he is <u>alone</u> in this creation (2:24). Even though he has a body, he is <u>alone</u> in the visible world, and is not just "a body among other bodies". Man is <u>alone</u> because he has consciousness and awareness. He knows the meaning of his own body because he experiences a unique and personal solitude.

Man's Unique Task

This second chapter also describes man's task. Before man was created "There was no one to till the ground or to make channels of water springing out of the ground to irrigate the whole land." (2:5-6). These words correspond to God's command in the first chapter. "Fill the earth and subdue it and have dominion ..." (1:28). The second chapter says specifically that only man can carry out this work of transforming the earth to care for man's needs. Dominating the earth lies only within man. This human activity belongs to the very definition of man and to his unique state of "being alone." *October 24, 1979*

7. LEARNING FROM THE TREE OF KNOWLEDGE

Superiority Based on Activity

Anthropology says that consciousness of the body is connected with man's discovery of the complexity of his structure. Genesis expresses this truth differently, "The Lord God formed man of dust from the ground and breathed into his nostrils the breath of life, and man became a living being." (2:7). Man is a "living being" who distinguishes himself from all other living beings. He does this because he is "capable of tilling the earth" (2:5) and subduing it (1:28). Consciousness of human superiority begins immediately. It is based on this typical human behavior and on man's intuition of his own body.

Perceiving By Experiencing

It is best to set aside anthropological complexity, because Genesis shows man perceiving the meaning of his body based upon his personal experiences. Man's bodily structure permits him to be the author of truly human activity in which man expresses his personhood. Due to his consciousness and self-determination, man can see who he is and who he should be.

Placed Before the Mystery

With this fundamental understanding of his own body, man is placed before the mystery of the tree of knowledge. "You may freely eat of every tree of the garden, but of the tree of knowledge of good and evil you shall not eat, for on the day that you eat of it you shall die." (2:16-17) From his original solitude, man learned that his existence came from the Creator.

However, man could not understand God's words "You shall die," because the word "die" was a completely new one. His human consciousness had no experience of this reality. The word appeared to him as a radical antithesis of all he had received from the Creator. Man contrasted the meaning of death with the life he had enjoyed so far. These words conveyed to man his dependence in existing, that he was a limited being who was liable to non-existence.

Man's Choice

"On the day that you eat it you shall die", raises the problem of death in a conditional way. Man had to discover their meaning in his own inner solitude. From these words, man learned that he could choose to enter death (the antithesis of created life) and make death and dying part of his experience. Man should have understood that this tree had roots, not just in the Garden of Eden, but also in his own humanity. He should have known that the tree concealed a new dimension of loneliness, greater than the loneliness which man had experienced in naming the animals.

A Deeper Loneliness

Experiencing solitude in the middle of the animals showed man that the invisible world determines him more than the visible.

10

Now, this choice between life and death (2:17) shows that man's body and all of humanity is destined for a heavenly existence. This alternative between death and immortality enters immediately into the definition of man. It belongs to "the beginning" and has meaning for the theology of the body.   *October 31, 1979*

8. THE UNIQUE JOY OF THE SECOND CREATION

From Aloneness to Companionship
"It is not good for man to be alone" (2:18) is a prelude to the creation of woman. The first chapter does not describe the problem of original solitude but merely states "male and female, he created them" (1:27). The second chapter, however, portrays man as alone in the material world.

Being Male and Female
Corporality and sexuality are distinct attributes of man. First, the man is seen as a "body," (a deeper subjective reality) before being described as a male or female. The original solitude of man is prior to the original unity of man and woman, (which is based on their being male or female, the two ways of "being a body.") Although the language is mythical, it helps us to discover a deeper meaning.

The second chapter stresses the creative action of God which makes "man" (expressed in Hebrew by "Adam") "male and female" (expressed in Hebrew by "is " and "issah"). This description corresponds to the process of human consciousness. First, God says that man should not be alone (2:8). Later, the text says that man experiences his own aloneness (2:20). God then puts man into a sleep and forms woman from his rib (2:21-22).

Quite a Sleep!
Let us consider this "sleep". In modern psychology, "sleep" often denotes a sexual content. The Genesis account goes much deeper. Man falls into a sleep and wakes up "male" and "female." Sleep, here, seems to be a return to non-being, a return to the moment before creation. This sleep allows man to emerge again, this time in his double unity of male and female. Man falls

into this sleep with a desire to find a being like himself. He dreams of a "second self." By this "sleep" man's solitude is broken and he awakens as male and female.

The Woman
The woman being formed "with a rib" shows the homogeneity of both sexes, especially of the body. Man expresses this clearly in words said to the woman but referring to his humanity, "This at last is bone of my bones and flesh of my flesh" (2:23). God had fulfilled His promise that he would make "a helper fit for him" (2:18). This bodily homogeneity is evident because she is called woman, taken from man (2:23). On seeing the woman, man expresses tremendous joy in the creation of this second human being, this second "self." These words establish the original unity of mankind because the woman is immediately accepted by the man as a fit helper for his tasks.

November 7, 1979

9. SOLITUDE –
MAKING THE MAN READY FOR A PARTNER

Unity and Duality
While this first couple has a unity, (a common sharing in the same human nature), their masculinity and femininity shows the duality of that nature. Although man was created as a particular value for God (who saw that all was good), man was also created as a particular value for himself and for others. Through the attraction of masculine for feminine, the unity of man overcomes the barrier of his solitude. From this attraction comes the unity of mankind, which we will call the "communion of persons."

A Decisive Opening For the Communion of Persons
In solitude, the man acquired a personal consciousness, distinguishing himself from all other living beings, and becoming open to another being like himself. This opening is decisive for man. It leads him to discover an adequate relationship in another human person and to look forward to a communion with that person.

12

"Communion" is a better word than "community", because it indicates a helping relationship. "Communion" is a "person beside a person", and a person "for" a person. Man, in his solitude was ready for this relationship. In fact, this communion depends upon the fact that they both realize their distinction from other living beings (a "double solitude"). They realized they were "helpers", able to give to each other what no other living being could give. Their relationship was only possible because they knew themselves as individuals and yet chose to be together.

God-like By Communion

Although made in God's image, man becomes even more like God by his communion with the woman. God Himself is a communion of persons. In the mystery of his original solitude, man possessed this deep unity because he was male and female, created for a communion of persons. Right from the beginning, man (male and female), is linked with the blessing of fertility and human procreation (1:28).

The heart of this study of the body is the text, "Bone of my bone and flesh of my flesh" (2:23). In saying these words, man identified what made the couple visibly similar and which manifested their common humanity.

Humanity Revealed by the Body

Man had contact with many "bodies," giving each a name. When he said "flesh of my flesh" he indicated that the woman's body revealed her humanity. Man is a person who is similar to God even in his body. The theology of the body is a theology of sex, of masculinity and femininity. "The two will be one flesh" (2:24) shows the original meaning of unity which will have an ethical dimension (cf, Christ's response to the Pharisees) and a sacramental dimension (cf Paul's words to the Ephesians) because the human "body" calls for a "communion of persons." "Bone of my bone and flesh of my flesh" (2:23) shows that man understands that human bodies can be mutually enriching. This deeper understanding establishes an inalienable norm for a theological understanding of man.

November 14, 1979

10. CHOOSING TO BECOME "ONE FLESH"

Enriched by Sexual Differences

We understand man's original unity by realizing that he chooses to move into a "communion" of persons. These are man's two complementary dimensions. "Being alone" and "being in communion" are man's two ways of being conscious of the meaning of the body. Man's self-knowledge passes through his/her femininity and masculinity and is confirmed in the presence of the other. Sex constitutes the person as a "he" or a "she." Man is enriched by being masculine and feminine, a teaching expressed by the phrase "bone of my bones and flesh of my flesh" (2:23).

The Blessing of Fertility and the Conjugal Act

Because they are male and female, they can become one flesh. This allows the couple to submit their humanity to the blessing of fertility. The expression "to become one flesh" shows both the full dimension of man and of his communion of persons.

"A man cleaves to his wife and they become one flesh," shows that man and woman rediscover the mystery of creation in every conjugal act. They return to that original union, described by the phrase "bone of my bones and flesh of my flesh". By the conjugal act, the couple relives the original experience of man emerging from solitude and discovering his own humanity.

Human sex is more than an instinctual bodily act. In the conjugal act, man surpasses the limits of his own solitude and assumes the body of a "second self" as one's own.

United By Choice

Through their bodies, masculine and feminine, men and women are led to this union of persons which is established by their mutual choice of a conjugal relationship. Because man needs self-knowledge to choose, he must have a mature consciousness that the body is made for mutual self-giving.

"By cleaving to his wife", a man rediscovers the significance of the body and renews the mystery of creation in its original depth. Woman is "taken out of man" as "flesh of his flesh" and she becomes, through man, both wife and mother.

14

Procreation reproduces the mystery of creation itself and proves that the unity of man and woman is inherent in the mystery of creation. *November 21, 1979*

11. UNDERSTANDING ORIGINAL INNOCENCE BY LATER EXPERIENCES

The Importance of the Original Experiences

These experiences of man's pre-history contain a meaning which is at the root of every human experience. They have an extraordinary character even though little attention is paid to them. Because revelation highlights these primordial experiences, we can discover the <u>extraordinary</u> side of <u>the ordinary</u>, and the absolute originality of the "male - female human being".

We must realize that, in these two chapters, man is experiencing his body on the threshold of his "historical experience". This helps us to understand the meaning of <u>original nakedness</u>, (one of the key elements of the original revelation). Original nakedness, (described in 2:25) is just as important as original solitude (2:20) and original unity (2:23) and is key to a full understanding of the theology of the body.

Their Original Personal Experience

"Naked and not ashamed" describes the couple's state of consciousness and their mutual reciprocal experience. This precise description of their experiences, although "pre-scientific," corresponds to modern anthropology which refers to the "experience of shame." When Christ spoke of "in the beginning", He established the continuity between the pre-historical and historical experiences of man. That they "were naked and yet not ashamed" forces us to look back into man's original innocence.

Later, Genesis describes a "nakedness with shame", "<u>Then</u> the eyes of both were opened and they knew they were naked" (3:7). <u>Then</u> means a new moment. This new situation begins because they have failed the first test of obedience. This new moment implies a different experience of their bodies because "shame" was not part of their original experience. "They were naked but they were not ashamed" does not mean that they didn't

15

realize they were naked. It is the experience of shame that is new. They do not pass from "not knowing" to "knowing". The change is in their personal experience of shame.

A Different Relationship

God says, "Who told you that you were naked?" (3:11) and asks "Have you eaten of the tree of which I commanded you not to eat?" (3:11). By sin, man has been changed in his relationship to God and to other creatures. He is now afraid of God. The man says, "I heard the sound of you in the garden and I was afraid because I was naked." (3:10) This text dramatically portrays the new relationship between man and woman. They have crossed over the border from innocence to sinfulness. We can reconstruct the original meaning of nakedness by studying this special experience of shame. *December 12, 1979*

12.   NAKED, INNOCENT, AND WITHOUT SHAME

Analyzing the Experience of Shame

Shame is a complex, fundamental experience. By shame, the person experiences a fear regarding his/her "second self" (as man before woman). This "fear for one self" shows the need for affirmation and acceptance. Shame is a complex experience which keeps the other person away. Yet, at the same time, shame seeks an acceptable basis to draw them closer into a personal relationship.

Shame has a fundamental significance in the ethics of the man - woman relationship. It expresses the essential rules for the "communion of persons". Shame touches upon the person's own original solitude. It was absent in the beginning experience and this absence was not just a lack of development. Genesis does not describe a primal or childhood experience. "They were not ashamed" (2:25) expresses a full, conscious understanding of the body.

Lessons From Original Nakedness

Shame appears when the original fullness is lost and the need for modesty begins. Therefore, we must explore that fullness which was present in the state of original nakedness. Man's

16

"original solitude" happened when he could not identify himself with the world of living beings. This "non-identification" paved the way for a full discovery of his own humanity through the help of another human being. The couple arrived at knowing their oneness as human persons through their bodies, "flesh of my flesh". Nakedness, therefore, corresponds to a full consciousness of the body's meaning.

Innocent Knowledge and Personal Communication

Man and woman were given to each other in a state of nakedness and they perceived their nakedness before they were complicated by "knowledge of good and evil". There was an original "innocence of knowledge", (naked and not ashamed). By their human inner life, the couple enjoyed a fullness of interpersonal communication. They were naked and yet not ashamed. Their communication was deeply personal and based upon their common union.

Communication Through Nakedness

The human body, although external, expresses this inner "personal, human self". The body manifests man. Only through the body can man and woman communicate. Understanding this full communication of persons allows us to understand original nakedness. This text speaks of a human experience which is outside of the limits of shame and through which interpersonal communication develops. "They were not ashamed" shows an affirming of the other person. The exterior perception of one another in full nakedness corresponds to the way God sees them. Man is naked (1:17) and realized it only after sin (3:7-10).

December 19, 1979

13. MAN ALONE CAN SEE CREATION AS GOD'S GIFT

Seeing As God Saw

Before knowing that they were naked, man and woman participated in the vision of God. They saw that everything He made was good (1:31).

Their nakedness signifies all the original good, the "pure value" of humanity as male and female and the "pure value" of the body and sex. There is no interior opposition between the spiritual and sensible, or between the person and the sexual determination of male and female. They see more fully because they see with an interior gaze which creates the full intimacy of persons.

Intimacy "Before Shame"

Shame brings a limitation to their personal intimacy. They became disturbed and even threatened by the sight of a naked body. Before shame, this couple enjoyed a reciprocal complementarity of male and female. They communicated as persons through their masculinity and femininity. Having this special understanding of their bodies, they are a gift for each other. Nakedness provided a full vision of their nuptial communion in which the couple knew clearly the meaning of their bodies.

"In the Image of God"

By describing the original meaning of solitude, unity and nakedness of man, these first two chapters provide the foundation for an adequate understanding of the human person. Genesis says that man was made "in the image of God" and provides all the essential elements to explain this phrase "in the image of God". Man and woman are really two different ways in which God's image is imprinted upon the human bodies "from the beginning."

Revealed As Created

Genesis frequently states that God "created". This provides a new criterion to help us understand original solitude , unity and nakedness. When Jesus also used the word "created", He asked us to see the theology of the body as part of the mystery of creation.

Receiving the Gift

God is love and the words "God saw what He had made, and behold it was very good" show God's nature. By calling everything "into existence from nothingness" God reveals Himself as a "radical giver". Within every creature is this sign of God's love. However, "giving" requires someone to receive, and demands a relationship. This relationship with God emerges only in the creation of man, who is made "in the image of God".

Only Man Can Understand

God's giving in creation only has a meaning for man. All creation was given to man. Although all creatures came from nothingness, only man can understand that it was God who created. Only man can respond to the gift. Man received this world as a gift and the world received man as a gift. Created man also received woman as a gift. *December 19, 1979*

14. THE EXHILARATING EXPERIENCE OF HAVING A PARTNER

A Missing Good

Did man really understand creation as a gift? Although man was in original happiness, he was "alone". This shows that something was lacking in his understanding. In fact, for the first time, Genesis describes a lack of a good. "It is not good for him to be alone" and "I will make him a helper". Among all the animals, man could not find "a suitable partner" with whom he could have a relationship of mutual giving.

"Alone" and "Helper"

The adjective "alone" and the noun "helper" are the key words to understand the phrase "made in the image of God" (which is the essence of the human person). If left "alone", man cannot realize completely his essence of existing "with someone", and/or of existing "for someone." Creation shows that this existing "with and for someone" is the norm of human existence. "Alone" and "helper" show that relationship and a communion of persons are fundamental for man. Relationship is the fulfillment of man's original solitude.

This fulfillment is exhilarating. Awaking from sleep and seeing the woman, the man expresses his joy, "This at last is bone of my bone and flesh of my flesh." (2:23). This beginning experience shows man's process of individuation. Man lived in original solitude (in the presence of all other creatures) until the woman was created.

Study of Person and Body-Sex

An adequate study of man requires that both "person" and "body-sex." be studied simultaneously. Otherwise, we would cover over the light contained in the revelation of the body. Creation is deeply connected with that beginning joy of existing as male and female. When man exclaimed "this is bone of my bone and flesh of my flesh" (2:23) he affirmed the human identity of the woman and said "Here is a body that expresses the human person."

Emerges From Solitude

The body reveals the "living soul" which God breathed into him (2:7). Because of this "living soul" man was originally "alone". He emerges from this solitude only by <u>the mutual gift</u> of the woman. This is expressed in the human body, with its masculinity and femininity.

The feminine body manifests the reciprocity and communion of persons. It witnesses to love as the source of creation. Masculinity and femininity are a sign that creation is a gift. In this way, sex enters into the theology of the body.

Nuptial Meaning

This beginning happiness is "nuptial," and is connected with the revelation and discovery of the body. This nuptial meaning of the body is shown by man being "male and female" (2:23), by their conjugal unity (2:24), and by their nakedness without mutual shame (2:25). God's giving in creation foreshadows the original consciousness of man who also experiences a mutual giving . Their "nakedness without shame" shows the fullness of their giving.

Man's Inner Sexual Freedom

The purpose of masculinity and femininity is for the couple "to become one flesh" (2:24), an action which will bring humanity into the blessing of procreation promised in Gen. 1:28. "To be naked and not ashamed" also shows that man is "free from the constraint of his own body and sex" even though he is aware of his sexuality and procreative powers.

Originally, man had an interior freedom from the sexual instinct. This term now implies an inner constraint which stimulates fertility in the lower species. In Genesis, procreation is part of a free personal choice. Human sexuality is raised above the animal level to the level of the "image of God" and of the person.

January 9, 1980

15. ENJOYING THE FULL TRUTH OF THEIR BODIES

Man's Full Freedom

Creation shows that man has the full truth of his body and sex. He has full freedom from inner constraints of the body and sex. They were "naked," with the freedom of the gift. The human body, with its sex (masculinity and femininity) is not just a source of procreation (as in the animal world) but has nuptial attributes, capable of expressing love. Vatican Council II said that man is the only creature whom God willed "for his own sake" and man "can fully discover his true self only in a sincere giving of himself" (GS 24). To be a "sincere gift of themselves" human persons must possess a full freedom which comes only from a mastery of oneself.

Enjoying Truth

Being naked and yet shameless reveals the freedom which makes possible a mutual "experience of the body." Because the couple is free, they can enjoy the whole truth of creation. They have an interior freedom which enables them to find one another and mutually accept one another. The woman is God's mystery in her femininity and the man, in his masculinity. They receive one another "for their own sake"

Fully Affirmed

When a person truly gives himself, his body reveals much more than the physical dimension of sexuality. Through their bodies, the couple show that they are willed for their own sake. They are persons, unique and unrepeatable. The person is affirmed

21

because their gift is accepted and their reciprocity creates a true "communion of persons."

Although coming from within the person, this communion comprises their exterior life. "They were not ashamed" indicates the subjective experience of this gift. The two human "egos" reveal the mystery of their first exhilarating meeting. This original happiness has "surprising theological and anthropological content" because, in his earthly history, man always seeks to recapture this "theme" of his own existence.

Revealing the Human Person

After sin, man's body retains its "nuptial meaning". Human history, however, will be quite different from this original happiness. The body's original nuptial meaning will suffer from many distortions. Therefore, the true nuptial meaning needs to be revealed in its full simplicity, so we can link the mystery of creation to the "redemption of the body" (Rom. 8).

No Sin – As Yet

As of yet, we have not entered the sinful stage of historical man. For now, the body's nuptial meaning is exhilarating, the great gift of creation which reveals the human person. This nuptial meaning shows that the person is created for himself and can discover himself only in a sincere giving.

January 16, 1980

16.   RECONSTRUCTING THE EXPERIENCE OF ORIGINAL INNOCENCE

Communicating Holiness

Creation is a radiation of love. It creates all that is good. This can be perceived in the exhilaration of original happiness. "Consistent giving" is rooted in the deepest parts of man's conscious and subconscious. These early chapters speak also of "grace", God communicating His holiness and giving man a special state of "spiritualization". Because man emerged from love and even initiated love, his happiness is "irrevocable" despite subsequent sin and death. Christ preached this irreversible love of the Creator.

22

edit: conscious afflicted and blocked temporarily.

Original Justice

In this beginning, man and woman do not know shame. Man was immune from shame due to love. This immunity reveals the mystery of man's original innocence, before he knew good and evil. By creation, man participated in grace, a share in God's own inner life (the interior source of original innocence). Theology calls this "original justice," the state of man before sin.

Original Innocence

Man's awareness of the meaning of the body reveals his unique state of original innocence. The Bible has many later texts of a shame, (or even ignominy) which accompanied nakedness. Therefore, the sentence "They were naked and yet not ashamed" is never repeated after sin.

Innocence was a mysterious grace given to the human heart which enabled the man and the woman to make a disinterested gift of self. Although sin has separated historical man from original innocence, theology can rediscover original innocence. In man's sinfulness, theology discovers a contrast with original innocence, especially through the experience of shame (which originally was excluded by innocence).

Original Righteousness

Through original innocence both man and woman could see creation as God's gift, especially in their own mutual giving. Innocence describes their own hearts and indirectly reveals human moral conscience. This was original righteousness, man's conscience before the knowledge of good and evil.

Exhilarating Because Innocent

From our sinful historical perspective, we can construct a picture of original innocence, (the reciprocal experience of the body with its nuptial meaning). Both innocence and happiness are two convergent parts of man's existence. The original exhilarating experience of happiness was due to original innocence, which is a "purity of heart" that preserves the inner faithfulness. This inner truth brings about a tranquil conscience. It precedes the knowledge

of good and evil and allows the nuptial meaning of the body to lead
to this human exhilarating experience.   *January 30, 1980*

17.   WELCOMING AND ACCEPTING –
GIVING AND RECEIVING

An Exchange Facilitated By Innocence

"This at last is flesh of my flesh" reveals the exhilarating
experience of the first encounter of male and female.   This
experience is rooted in their inner freedom and their original
innocence.   Freedom and innocence facilitated the gift of the body
because there was innocence in their mutual experience of their
bodies.   "Being naked and without shame" shows this innocence
which inspires their mutual exchange of the gift.   Their exchange
consists in a reciprocal "receiving" and "accepting" of the other.

Welcoming and Accepting

This "acceptance" and "welcome," in their mutual
nakedness sustains the gift and deepens their mutual dignity.   It
corresponds to God's will, because He made them "male and
female".   Not "to welcome" or "to accept" would be a deprivation,
a changing, and a reduction of the other to "an object for myself."

An extorting of the gift and reducing the other to "an object
for myself" will mark the beginning of shame.   This is a threat to
the intimacy and shows the interior collapse of innocence.   By "not
being ashamed", the two persons preserved the innocence of their
"giving" and "accepting".

Man and Woman – Giving and Receiving

The woman is given to the man by the Creator and she is
received by the man due to his original innocence.   The way man
accepts her is his first "giving".   By giving herself, the woman
"rediscovers herself," because she has been accepted· and
welcomed by the man.   She finds herself by giving herself and by
being accepted "for her own sake", in the whole truth of her body,
sex and femininity.   She reaches full possession of herself and
becomes the source of new giving.

24

Dynamism of the Gift

Edit: possession of God's exhileration within himself and His stamped image, or image of God rooted in Himself. B.A.K.

"Finding oneself by giving" results in an even deeper acceptance and a more intense awareness. The man seems to have the duty of receiving the woman because she is entrusted to him. By receiving the woman, the man enriches her and is himself enriched. By receiving her and then giving of his own body, man reaches a deep "possession of self." When received by the woman, the man is enriched in his own masculinity. This becomes a source of a deeper enrichment for both. This exchange increases the giving and accepting of each other.   *February 6, 1980*

18.   ORIGINAL INNOCENCE – HELPING US TO UNDERSTAND OUR SINFUL STATE

A "Spiritualization" of Man

Chapter Two highlights a human subjectivity which indicates a "spiritualization" of man (an existence which is quite different from historical man). This original innocence shows a different arrangement of man's inner powers and a different relationship of body and soul. There is a different inner proportion between sensitivity, spirituality and affectivity than is present in historical man. Originally, man had a higher degree of sensitivity to the gifts of the Spirit. The teachings of theology and the Church's Magisterium help us to understand these conditions of man's original innocence.

Ethics and Original Innocence

When Christ said, "Have you not read that he who made them from the beginning, made them male and female?" He ordered us to examine this mystery of creation. This is true even though a barrier now separates us from how the original couple experienced masculinity/femininity, and how they gave themselves to each other. Although that original state of innocence is lost, we believe that the "state of fallen nature is now redeemed". Knowing the connection between the fallen nature of mankind and the original nature of innocence is important. By defining this

25

connection, we can see the permanent human and theological roots which are needed for an ethics of the body.

At the beginning of his own history, man was aware of the nuptial meaning of masculinity or femininity. Christ said that we must construct our moral truths based on how it was "in the beginning". God always creates us as He did in the beginning, that is, male and female. Understanding the nuptial meaning that was "in the beginning" is absolutely necessary to know who man is, who he should be, and how he should mold his own activity.

Sin Destroys the Ethical Norm

In the beginning, the man and woman were created "to become one flesh". This is the great creative perspective. Man's existence is continually renewed by procreation, or "self-reproduction". However, before becoming man and wife, the two persons were created as brother and sister, sharing the same humanity.

The communion of persons began by free choice. They chose to live as man and wife. They both grew as "persons" through their bodies and through their nakedness without shame. Unfortunately, after sin, they will cease to be a "disinterested gift" and will recognize that "they are naked", as shame springs up in their hearts. Only original innocence can manifest the perfect system of ethical norms. *February 13, 1980*

19. THE FIRST NUPTIAL FEAST –
SUBJECTIVE BLISS AND GIFT

Mutually Enjoying the Gift

The lack of shame shows that the woman was not merely an object for man. Their interior innocence made it possible for them to be naked and yet not be reduced to objects. "Being without shame" shows that they mutually enjoyed the nuptial meaning of their bodies. As persons, they used their freedom and their interior riches. Their mutual oneness excludes reducing the other to an object, and gives us a subjective profile of their love.

Now – Difficult to Discover

When original innocence was lost by sin, man no longer had this grace. Now, he has difficulty in discovering the true nuptial meaning of his body. However, this nuptial meaning remains inscribed in the human heart (a distant echo of original innocence) and continues to form man's inner truth. After sin, however, shame is needed. Only through shame can man rediscover his role as the guardian of the other person. Shame never allows a person to be reduced to an object.

Man – The First Sacrament

For now, we are still at the threshold of man's earthly history (before this couple had any knowledge of good and evil). Man still appears as the highest expression of the divine gift. He has an interior understanding by which he transcends and dominates his "visibility." He also has a primordial awareness of the nuptial meaning of his body and sees himself as the primordial sacrament. He transmits to the visible world the mystery hidden in God from all eternity.

By his visible masculinity and femininity man is the sacrament of creation. The body alone is capable of bringing the invisible and the spiritual into the visible world. By his body, man becomes a visible sign of God's plan. The sacrament of marriage, therefore, is the beginning sacrament, the first sign that God is Creator.

The First Feast of Holiness

Being naked and not ashamed shows that holiness entered the world with man. The sacrament of the world and of man in the world, come from the holiness of God. Because man knows he is a subject of holiness, original innocence allows man to express himself with his body. "This at last is flesh of my flesh" narrates the first feast of humanity. Although the specter of sin and death will soon come over this feast, that first feast still gives us hope. The first fruit of creation is life and not death, and the mystery of creation is not the destruction of the body but the "call to glory" (Rom. 8:30).   *February 20, 1980*

27

20. THE TWO MEANINGS OF "TO KNOW"

Revealing the Original Drama
By the time Christ spoke, man's beginning innocence had already been shattered by the "mystery of sin" and the "mystery of death". Nevertheless, His words lead us back beyond the limits of sinful man and show the continuity between the state of innocence and the state of sin. Genesis reveals this drama of man's origins.

Knowledge and Fertility
This leads to our final analysis, that of knowledge and of procreation." Although closely connected to the blessing of fertility, this knowledge is also part of sin and death (Gen: C.3).

Genesis teaches that historical man has a distorted meaning of the human body. Genesis defines the conjugal union as "knowledge". "Adam knew Eve his wife and she conceived..." (4:1). By using the word "knowledge", Genesis teaches that the conjugal relationship of man and woman enters into the sphere of persons. Although Genesis speaks only of the man knowing the woman (stressing the man's activity), there is certainly a reciprocity of knowledge (cf 4:17 and 4:25). Let us recall that Mary said to the angel Gabriel, "I know not man" (Lk1:34).

Being Known and Revealed
The word "knew," shows the intention of the man. It reveals the conjugal life in which man and woman become "one flesh." The Bible uses the word "knew" to reveal the deepest essence of married life. By becoming "one flesh," man and woman experience the meaning of their body. While remaining two distinct subjects, they become a mutual subject of the conjugal act. In the conjugal act they reveal themselves to each other, and are given to each other to be "known by the other".

In Genesis (4:1-2) they are "given" to each other. This conjugal union contains a new discovery of the meaning of the body. The persons are not passive objects nor are they determined by nature. They are man and woman, given to each other as persons. Sex decides man's bodily individuality and defines his

28

personal identity. In the conjugal act, this unrepeatable female-male person is known. This conjugal knowledge reaches into the deepest roots of the identity of man and woman, which they owe to their sex.   *March 5, 1980*

21. MOTHERHOOD –
A MYSTERY HIDDEN WITHIN THE WOMAN

Conjugal Knowing

By the power of knowing, man distanced himself from the animal world and affirmed himself as "person" (2:20). The conjugal union (4:1) is also an act of knowing, (not a passive acceptance of being determined). This sexual knowing is a reciprocal discovery and is the basis for the unity of man and woman.

The Revelation of Motherhood

Man confirms the meaning of Eve, who was "the mother of all the living" (3:20). According to Genesis, man is "knower" and woman is the "known". The depth of her femininity is within her body and her sex. Femininity, (according to Gen 4:1) is completely revealed by motherhood. "She conceived and bore…" (4:1). The woman now stands before the man as mother. This reveals a new mystery, the generative and fatherly meaning of the male body.

Potentiality for Procreation

Genesis contains the primary contents of a theology of the body. Although woman is constituted differently from man, this difference is manifested only partially in the external form of her body. Within her, lies the potentiality for maternity and for the procreation of a new person. She fulfills this inner gift as the man knows her and she conceives.

Procreation means that the husband and wife know each other in their child, a third person who comes from both. In this new man the spouses recognize themselves. Their knowledge of each other now has a living content and their level of "self-conscious and self-determination" reaches fatherhood and motherhood.

29

The Mystery of Motherhood

The entire body of the woman, (with its perennial attractiveness) is closely allied with motherhood. Luke's gospel celebrates "the womb that bore you and the breasts that you sucked" (11:27), a eulogy of the feminine body and of creative love. When Eve understood this maternal maturity of her body, she exclaimed, "I have begotten a man with the help of the Lord" (4:1).

These words have a theological depth. By procreation, the conceived man already assumes his human aspects while in the womb. The words "this is bone of my bone and flesh of my flesh" (2:23) is confirmed by "I have begotten a man." Eve knows that the mystery of creation is renewed and that God participates in human generation. She knows that she has conceived..."with the help of the Lord." These first parents teach clearly that even after sin, every man is born in the image of God.

Dignity of Human Generation

Despite the deep differences between man's states of original innocence and of historical sinfulness, this "image of God" provides continuity and unity. By knowing, the first man took possession of the visible world. The same man, male and female, by knowing each other, renew the existence of man in " the image of God". This happens every time a man and woman transmit life "with the help of the Lord". In describing this first birth of man, Genesis says everything about the dignity of human generation.

March 12, 1980

22. THE PROCREATION GIFT – NOW SUBJECT TO DEATH

Bone of My Bones

By conjugal knowledge, man gives existence to a new humanity. By generating new life, man completes the biblical cycle of "knowledge-generation".

God gave all of creation to man as its master. "Subdue the earth and have dominion over it" (1:28). God's command, "Be fruitful and multiply" (1:28), shows that man and woman would now give existence to other men/women. The child is "bone of my bones and flesh of my flesh" (2:24), and the couple is literally "carried off" together, possessed by a new humanity which their mutual knowledge conceived.

Knowing But Not Possessing

Although biblical knowledge is a possession, it is not the same as Eros. In the original revelation, the idea of man possessing the woman as an object, and vise versa, is not present. Sex was a selfless, mutual gift. Because of sin, man and woman need great effort to recapture this original meaning.

Birth and Death

Genesis (C.3) shows clearly that this cycle of knowledge-generation is now subject to suffering and death. "I will greatly multiply your pain in childbearing" (3:16) and "You are dust and unto dust you shall return" (3:19). Genesis reveals the body's generative meaning and also the presence of death in the body. Knowing this, Adam calls his wife "Eve" because she is "the mother of all the living" (3:20).

This experience of death will always be part of human history. Man has broken the covenant and is now detached from the tree of life, "Now, let him not put forth his hand and take also of the tree of life, and eat, and live forever" (3:21). Life is not taken away but is restricted by death and hurt by hereditary sinfulness. Life is given to man as a task in the cycle of conception, birth and death.

The Beginning of History

"Adam knew his wife and they conceived" (4:1) marks the very beginning of man's history. Every person carries this mystery in the generative meaning of his body. Unfortunately, Gen 4:1-2 is silent of the relationship between the generative meaning and the nuptial meaning of the body, but this question will be raised again with the appearance of shame.

Aware of Birth and Death

When Adam and Eve conceive, human history begins. They are aware of the generative meaning of their bodies, with masculinity concealing fatherhood and femininity concealing motherhood. (In light of that meaning, Christ will give his answer to the question of divorce.)

Man also is aware of death which comes to everybody. In human history, the knowledge-generation cycle struggles with death and overcomes it. Life refuses to surrender to death because man always chooses to go beyond his own solitude to procreate offspring. In spite of suffering, disappointment, and even the prospect of inevitable death, man continues to place first this knowledge of generation which is his sharing in the vision of God who saw that "it was very good" (1:31).   *March 26, 1980*

23. ONLY "THE BEGINNING" REVEALS THE POSSIBILITIES OF HUMAN LIFE

The Clarity of "the Beginning"

Because Christ referred twice to "the beginning" these chapters have tried to examine that "beginning". This is the first inheritance of every person, the first description of human identity, and the first certain source of man's vocation "in the image of God". Christ's answer concerned the divorce law of Moses, and in answering contemporary questions, Christ would certainly refer us again to "the beginning"

Responding to Modern Questions

Examining the beginning reveals the nature of man's identity in the mysteries of creation and of redemption, upon which the Church bases its teaching. Pope Paul VI, in Humanae Vitae referred to "the total vision of man", the perspective that Christ put forward to the Pharisees. Contemporary moral questions must be answered from this "total vision."

The Full Truth

Because our modern culture has developed a variety of disciplines, it has replaced this total vision by partial conceptions.

Individual disciplines focus on the human composite and not on "integral man". These disciplines make man an object of determined techniques instead of a subject responsible for his choices. In contrast to this modern approach, Christ wants each person to make decisions in the complete and original truth found only "in the beginning."

Because this "beginning" is at a pre-scientific level, it tells us little of the interior structure of the human organism. However, the text reveals a total vision of man in a simple and full way. Although modern science can teach us much about human sexuality in the bio-physiological sense, the total truth of man's sexual nature being personal and inter-personal is often lost in modern teachings.

A Full Theology

These ancient texts of Genesis are irreplaceable because they begin the "Theology of the Body". Later when the Word became flesh, the body entered theology by the main door. The mysteries of Christ's birth, death and rising became the definitive sources for the sacramentality of marriage.

This theology of the body is especially important for human persons who live in the sacrament of marriage. They need to know the nuptial and generative meaning of the body. Science gives information but only the Word of God can supply a complete revelation of the body's meaning.

April 2, 1980

Part Two
Christ's Sermon on the Mount

24. TRUTH –
LEADING TO A SUPERABUNDANT JUSTICE

The Basic Words

Christ said, "You have heard it was said, 'You shall not commit adultery': But I say to you that everyone who looks at a woman lustfully has already committed adultery with her in his heart." (Mt:5,27-28). By these words, Jesus revises the understanding of the moral law of the Old Covenant.

The Wider Context

Before speaking about "looking with lust", Jesus said, "Think not that I have come to abolish the law and the prophets. I have not come to abolish them but to fulfill them." (5:17). Later, Jesus said, "Whoever...does them (these commandments) and teaches them, shall be called great in the kingdom of heaven." (5:19). By "the kingdom of heaven", Jesus means eternal life.

A Greater Righteousness

Jesus' words, "Unless your righteousness exceeds that of the scribes and Pharisees, you will never enter the kingdom of God." (5:20), urge us not to interpret God's law in a human manner. This hinders the superabundant justice willed by God.

By condemning "adultery in the heart", Christ asked for a greater righteousness. By giving a clear understanding of the sixth commandment's foundation, Jesus provides the conditions which are needed to fulfill that commandment and bring about the "greater righteousness".

At the Heart of Ethics

By investigating the sixth commandment and the justice which must superabound within the person, we are at the heart of ethics, almost at the soul of human morality. Contemporary thinkers (e.g. Scheler) see the Sermon on the Mount as the great turning point in ethics, because morality is truly alive only when people actually live this superabundant justice. To live this way, the person needs an inner perception of values. Ethics must enter into the depth of the human person because moral values are connected with the person's inner dynamics.

Inner Action of the Person

When Jesus said, "Everyone who looks at a woman lustfully has already committed adultery with her in his heart." He joined the two commandments, "Thou shalt not commit adultery" and "Thou shalt not covet your neighbor's wife". His teaching highlights the inner act which is contained in any person's exterior action of adultery.

Old Testament Loopholes

This inner action is expressed visibly by adultery in which man and woman violate the law of matrimonial exclusiveness. Unfortunately, the Old Testament investigated this "act of the body" according to external criteria. It opened up various "loopholes". Jesus called these multiple compromises "hardness of heart" (Mt.19:8). God's commandments underwent a distortion because people kept the legal observances but did not abound in interior justice. By His words, Jesus deliberately shifts the question to the inner dimension. He appeals to the interior man, and his eloquence makes the norm very explicit.   *April 16, 1980*

25. RECAPTURING THE FULL MEANING OF "YOU SHALT NOT COMMIT ADULTERY"

Speaking to Modern Man

Jesus' words about adultery (Mt.5:27-28) are spoken to historical man, both those who were present and those who came after. Some modern men know these words, "You shall not commit adultery." Others, although ignorant of this commandment, have the law "written on his heart" (Rom.2:15). Historical man, at the very beginning of his earthly existence, found himself "inside the knowledge of good and evil and he knew his wife so that she conceived and bore" (Gen.4:1-2). This was according to God's plan, both in the state of original innocence and in the state of historical sinfulness.

Speaking to the "Interior Man"

By speaking to this "interior man", Jesus addresses everyone. Christ's words speak to man, who is "flesh", a male, in relationship to a woman who is female. "You shall not commit adultery." requires that this man find his true identity. This is linked to the nuptial and procreative meaning of his body.

Definitions of Christ's Words

Adultery happens when a man unites as "one flesh" with a woman who is not his wife, and vice versa. "Adultery in the heart", happens when a man "looks at a woman lustfully". He directs his desire toward a woman who is not his wife, to unite with her as if she were his wife. This desire is expressed by the sense of sight, as in the case of David and Bathsheba (2Sm.11:2).

While focusing on sight, Christ's words do not say clearly whether the woman is single or married. Obviously, when a man looks at his own wife, he does not commit adultery "in his heart", because he cannot commit adultery with his wife. The conjugal act is lawful in their relationship and is in conformity with the moral law.

Christ, although referring equally to man and woman, deliberately speaks of a man "looking lustfully" to give a concrete example of the meaning given by God in creating the human body. His words help us arrive at a general truth about historical man.

April 23, 1980

26. BREAKING AWAY FROM THE FATHER – (1 John)

Three Forms of Lust

St. John outlines three forms of lust: "For all that is in the world, the lust of the flesh and the lust of the eyes and the pride of life, is not of the Father but is of the world, and the world passes away, and the lust of it, but he who does the will of God abides forever" (1John 2:16-1). John teaches that lust is "not of the Father", but is "of the world".

This three-fold lust (both "in the world" and "of the world"), is not from creation, but comes from the tree of knowledge of good and evil (Gen.2:17). This fruit came forth from sin. By sin, the "world" which God created has become the "world of lust" (1Jn.2:15-16).

Lust – Not of the Father

When John says that lust "is not of the Father but is of the world" his teaching corresponds with Genesis, where the origin of lust is clear. Christ's words lead us back to the threshold of authentic human experience, and His teachings about "the beginning" provide important elements in a study of man.

Obviously, John's teaching corresponds to Christ's words on adultery. Both reveal a truth about man, specifically the man who looks lustfully at a woman.

Need to Understand This Lustful Man

This look is explained by the fact that he is a "man of lust". The man (who looks) and the woman (as the object of his look) are part of the three-fold dimension of lust. We must know lust and this "lustful man" to understand Christ's words on adultery (Mt.5:27-28).

In Genesis, the man, male and female, first appears in original innocence. Then, he appears as one who has lost innocence, having broken his original covenant with his Creator (Gen. 3:1-5). In the key moment, man makes a fundamental choice against God's will and accepts the motivation of the tempter, "You will be like gods, who know good and evil." This motivation shows that man questioned God's original gift of creation. Man had received the whole world (including his own humanity, male and female) and was made in God's image. He then turned his back on the Creator (3:1-5) by questioning if creation really is an act of God's love. In doing so, he detached his heart from what "is of the Father" and there remained in him only what is "of the world"

Man's New State

A new state of human nature began. "Then the eyes of both were opened and they knew that they were naked and they sewed fig leaves together and made themselves aprons." (3:7). This sentence certainly speaks of the beginning of lust and of shame, which place a "limit" to personal communion.

By describing shame, Genesis shows the "frontier" between original innocence and man's sinfulness. Genesis (2:25) had said that they "were both naked and were not ashamed" but now it speaks of a shame connected with sin. This shame shows that what is in man and woman "is not of the Father, but of the world".

April 30, 1980

27. THE NEW EXPERIENCES OF FEAR AND SHAME

Shame and Fear

"They sewed fig leaves together and made themselves aprons." (3:7) speaks of the mutual shame of man and woman. This reaches their deepest level, and shakes the foundation of their existence. For this reason, they hid themselves when they heard the sound of the Lord God (3:8). The immediate fruit of the knowledge of good and evil was a fear of God which they had not previously experienced. Adam's words explain his experience, "I heard the sound of You in the garden and I was afraid because I was naked and I hid myself." (3: 9-10).

Revealing the True Cause

This is more than just a physical shame that is often associated with nakedness. Adam covers up the source of his fears. God reveals their true origin by asking, "Who told you that you were naked? Have you eaten of the tree of which I commanded you not to eat?" (3:11).

This precise dialogue reveals the depths of man's emotion. Nakedness and shame do not just refer to his body. They reveal a man deprived of his gift and alienated from God. Man was deprived of the original supernatural and preternatural gifts and suffered a loss in his original fullness. These deficiencies correspond to John's three forms of lust.

38

A Radical Change

The man said. "I was afraid because I was naked and I hid myself." Obviously his new state differs greatly from his original state and he has undergone a radical change from original nakedness without shame.

By his body, man first confirmed himself as a person. He surpassed all other living beings, and his body was a witness to his original solitude. Through masculinity and femininity, his body was the clear element in his communion with the woman. By accepting his body, man accepted the whole visible creation and guaranteed his dominion over all the earth (1:28).

Loss of Certainty

By sin, man lost this original certainty and his sense of participating in God's perception of the material world. Before sin, man had enjoyed living in the truth of his own body, because the Creator "saw that it was very good." (1:31) "I was afraid because I was naked and I hid myself." shows a collapse of man's original acceptance of his body and a shaking of his acceptance of the material world.

Now Earth Subdues Man

God's words to the woman concerning the pains of childbirth (3:16) and to the man concerning the lack of the earth's fertility and the difficulty of toil (3:1-19) predict a new hostility of the created world. Nature will resist man's toil and fatigue will affect the human body. The end of this toil is death, "to dust you shall return" (3:19).

"I was afraid because I was naked, and I hid myself" shows man is aware of his body's insecurity before the determinism of nature. Man also suffers from a "cosmic shame". Man, created to subdue the earth, is now subjected to the earth.   *May 14, 1980*

28. A NEW THREAT FROM WITHIN

Mutual Shame

Besides cosmic shame (toward God), another form of shame appears. This is caused by a deep disorder within man.

This shame is within the man and within his relationship to the woman. It causes them to hide their own bodies, removing the visible signs of masculinity and femininity.

Shame Within

Although this text about "making aprons" (3:7) seems to involve sexual shame, the earlier words, "I was afraid because I was naked" show a personal difficulty, independent of the other sex. Man's original unity is ruptured. He realizes that his body is no longer under the power of the Spirit which raised him to the level of God's image. Shame reveals the seeds of the inner human contradiction that will always accompany historical man. Paul writes, "I see in my members another law at war with the law of my mind." (Rom.7:22-23)

Shame is now within man, bringing an acute awareness of the fundamental unrest in all human existence. This original shame is fear, and announces an uneasiness of a conscience connected with lust.

The Body's Rebellion

The body is no longer subordinated to the spirit. It now resists the spirit and threatens the person's moral unity. Lust becomes a threat to self-mastery, because the man of lust cannot control his own body. His self-mastery is shaken to its foundations.

This immanent shame certainly has a sexual nature, and human sexuality highlights this interior imbalance. "They made aprons" (3:7) because the "man of lust" felt he had stopped being above the animals. A rupture took place in the integrity of those bodily parts which determine sexuality and which should lead to the personal communion of man and woman.

This immanent sexual shame is especially manifested in the presence of the opposite sex. Therefore, we can understand Christ's words about the man who "looks at a woman lustfully" (Mt. 5:27-28). Christ calls these lustful desires "adultery in the heart."

"From the World"

Shame recalls the moment when the first man closed himself to what came "from the Father" and opened himself to what came "from the world". Shame and lust always go together. Man is ashamed of his lust and of the effect which lust has upon his spirit.

Psychology and Bible

We must note that psychology and the Bible speak quite differently of desire and lust. For psychology, desire comes from a lack of something which is needed. The Bible (1John 2:16) says that lust comes from the fact that the human spirit is removed from its original simplicity. The original experience of man and woman underwent a radical transformation when shame and lust were born.

Shame has a double meaning. It reveals a threat to the value of the person but also acts to preserve that value. The human heart holds on to shame "so that the person is not used as an object of lust". We need to examine the human heart.   *May 28, 1980*

29. FROM "ONENESS" TO "CONFRONTATION"

Harmful Effects

Genesis shows that shame appeared in the mutual relationship of man and woman and was accompanied by lust. Original shame shows that lust had a harmful effect upon the communion of persons, (the task given them by God). This shame induces the couple to hide their bodies and their sexual differentiation. Their original capacity for sexual communion has been shattered. This radical change points to other negative changes in their relationship. Their mutual communion is upset, as if the body can no longer be its foundation. They have lost confidence that their bodies can be the basis for their relationship.

A Threshold of Confrontation

Although they continued to communicate with each other, the purity of their original experience disappears. An insuperable threshold limits their mutual giving. Their sexual diversity is now experienced as a mutual confrontation of persons. "They knew they were naked" (3:7) portrays the origin of shame and reveals its effects in man and woman.

This new state helps us to appreciate the value of the body's unifying meaning. We understand this "closure to one another" by comparing this state of sinfulness with original innocence, whereby they became "one flesh" (2:24). Their mutual shame shows that they lost their original certainty that the human body could unite them.

The Body Becomes an Obstacle

Shame also shows that man lost his sense of being "in the image of God". The masculine/feminine which had highlighted the body for a communion of persons, now focuses only on the sense experiences of sexuality. This is an obstacle to personal communion because both spouses hide their sexuality by making an apron.

This second experience of sex differs radically from the original gift and distinguishes lustful historical man from the original man. Lust of the flesh is harmful to that communion of persons which was assigned to man by God "from the beginning".

Shame Replaces Trust

Lust introduces a difficulty into the body's role. Because of lust, the couple hides those bodily parts which determine masculine/feminine. This shows a fundamental lack of trust and the collapse of the original relationship. Shame has replaced their absolute trust. By examining this shame, we can understand the boundary between the man of original innocence and the historical man of lust. *June 4, 1980*

30. SERIOUS CHANGES IN THE RELATIONSHIP

The Effects Upon the Woman

Genesis also describes other effects besides shame replacing the absolute trust. God speaks of the pain of childbirth, "I will greatly multiply your pain in childbearing; in pain you shall bring forth your children." God also describes her future, "Your desire shall be for your husband, and he shall rule over you." (3:16).

This incisive formulation describes a particular "disability" of the woman as compared with man. This is not a social disability or an inequality, but a disability which the woman will feel in her interpersonal communion with man.

"Your desire will be for your husband, and he shall rule over you." concerns the whole context of their relationship, not just the moment of their conjugal act. These words show a basic loss in the communion of persons which should make man and woman mutually happy by their reciprocal self-giving and by subordinating their union to the blessing of procreation.

Effects Upon Both

God's words to the woman echo a fuller experience of shame. The original exhilarating union is now distorted by the lust in the man's heart. Although these words are addressed to the woman, they are actually said to man and woman because both suffer from the change.

They are now more divided, opposed because of their masculinity/femininity and driven by an instinctive impulse to cover their bodies. Man, is now male or female rather than male and female. He is estranged from the original source of unity, (his own body), and finds himself opposed to the woman because of his body. Although this opposition does not destroy the conjugal act or its procreative effects, it seriously changes the joy of their union.

This human couple, created in innocence, is now different. While still called to unity, they are now threatened by the instability of their union. While still called and attracted to a communion of persons, they experience sexual shame and their desires for full communion in the conjugal act are not fulfilled.

The Three-Fold Lust

At the basis of this shame is the three-fold lust, "of the flesh, of the eyes and of the pride of life" (1Jn.2:16). "He shall rule over you." (3:16) shows the pride of life which changes the communion of persons. The other person becomes an object which can be desired by the lust of the eyes. These words explain the historical conflict of man with woman.   *June 18, 1980*

31. THE MANY POISONS OF LUST

Lust and Shame

"Your desire shall be for your husband and he shall rule over you" (3:16) clarifies and interprets this feeling of shame. Shame does not lie in the body, but in the deeper inner parts of the human spirit which knows that its lustful desires are insatiable.

This awareness of lust blames the body, and deprives the body of the simplicity of original innocence. Shame reveals the presence of lust because shame is meant to protect the body from the threefold lust. By shame, man and woman can almost remain in original innocence if they preserve themselves from lust.

The Authentic Union

"A man ... cleaves to his wife and they become one flesh." (2:24) shows the union of bodies in an authentic union. The union comes from a choice, his deliberate leaving of parents to be with a wife as "one flesh". This "sacramental" expression contrasts with the historical distortion of the relationship in which the man "shall be your master". The body continues to stimulate the desires for personal union ("Your desires shall be for your husband.") but directs them in the wrong way ("He shall rule over you.").

Effects of Lust

Lust directs these desires to the body in a way which destroys personal communion. Although the man feels intensely ashamed of his own body, "I was naked and I hid myself", yet, his impulse is to "dominate" the woman.

The woman, while experiencing this domination, also has an insatiable desire for a "possessing". She, too, changes the mutual relationship and wants to "possess" the man as an object of her desire. The woman's desire can even precede man's and give his desires impetus.

Although Genesis (3:16) and Jesus (Mt.5:27-28) speak of man as the one who desires, the woman also is moved by lust. Shame touches the innermost recesses of both sexes, although in different ways. All three forms of lust cloud the understanding of the nuptial meaning of the body. This true meaning of the body should determine the person's attitude and way of living. This is what Christ calls "the heart", the interior man.

The Body's Meaning – Distorted in History

The body has an objective significance and is, in a sense, "a-historical". We, however, must examine the man of "history". "Historical" means all the facts about man, facts of both sin and of salvation.

Historical man lives in a limitation caused by lust. This determines his attitudes and his way of living in the body. He is no longer in original innocence. This distortion and limitation is clearly seen in Adam and Eve. Through them, we discover their original communion as well as the distortion of their relationship by the presence of shame. We must reconstruct this distortion to truly understand lust. Genesis (C.3) provides the answers.

June 25, 1980

32. NOW – LOVE AND LUST DO BATTLE IN THE HEART

The Body – Limited By Concupiscence

The human body is the source of fertility and a means of expressing love. In expressing love, the body enters into a communion of persons, (which is an image of God). Concupiscence of the body, "that comes from the world", limits man's participation in this image of God and the human heart experiences this limitation. The mutual relations of masculinity and femininity no longer express the original joy of communion. They often remain only at the level of attraction, such as exists in the animal world.

In original innocence, the sexual attraction expressed this call to personal communion. After sin, this call is weakened and placed on a lower level. After sin, human sexuality became an almost "autogenous force", a "coercion of the body" which had its own dynamics and limited the experience of personal communion. "Your desire shall be for your husband, and he shall rule over you." shows this weakened and lower level.

Battlefield

The human body has "almost" lost the capacity to become a deep gift to the other. We say "almost" because this capacity can be recaptured by human love. The nuptial meaning of the body, although habitually threatened by concupiscence, has not been completely suffocated. However, the heart has become a battlefield between love and lust.

If lust dominates, the person becomes less sensitive to the gift of the other. This lust, which Christ speaks of (Mt.5:27-28), appears in many forms and is not always obvious. This lust is concealed, is passed off as love, changes its profile, and dims the clarity of the gift. Even so, we must not distrust the human heart, but keep it under control.

Lust Depersonalizes

Man is the "only creature on earth whom God has willed for his own sake" and the only creature who "can fully discover his true self only in a sincere giving of himself". Lust attacks this "sincere giving", deprives man of his dignity and depersonalizes him, making him an object for the other. Instead of being "together with the other" (the sacramental unity) the spouses become objects for each other's domination.

The body becomes more important than the person, and man becomes an object of concupiscence. The personal relationship is unilaterally reduced to the body and sex. Sexual relations no longer contain the full personal experiences and do not fully express personal communion.

Loss of Inner Freedom

Concupiscence causes the loss of inner freedom. It brings about a coercion of the body, reduces self-control and makes the inner freedom of giving impossible. Man can only become a gift if he controls himself. The beauty of the body is obscured when it becomes an object of lust. Concupiscence cannot promote personal communion because it doesn't unite but appropriates. The relationship of gift is replaced by a relationship of appropriation. This subtle point of the difference between authentic love and lust is considered in the next chapter.   *July 23, 1980*

46

33. APPROPRIATION VERSUS MUTUAL GIVING

Unilateral Appropriation

"Your desire shall be for your husband, and he shall rule over you." reveals how sin changed the original relationship of mutual giving into mutual appropriation. When a man sees a woman only as an object, he makes himself an object of appropriation and not a gift. This unilateral appropriation (which is indirectly bilateral) destroys personal communion because both human beings lose their inner freedom.

The Woman's Experience and Man's Duty

The text suggests that this happens most often at the expense of women. "Your desire shall be for your husband, and he shall rule over you.", finds a parallelism in Christ's words "Everyone who looks at a woman lustfully ...". These words do not stress the woman as the object, but highlight the truth that man "from the beginning" was to be the guardian of the mutual giving.

Man is responsible for accepting the woman as a gift (Gen.2:23-25), and making a bilateral exchange. Although both persons have responsibilities, man has a special duty to maintain this mutual exchange of gifts. Although women were marginalized when these scriptures were written, this truth is independent of those specific conditions. By lust, the body becomes a "place of appropriation", and the mutual belonging of the persons acquires a different meaning.

A Correct Use of "My"

The word "my" is used frequently in the Song of Songs and shows a personal analogy of a relationship which is formed by mutual belonging. (An analogy shows both a similarity and a dissimilarity.) "Belonging" presupposes a relationship of possession and ownership. This relationship is both objective and, above all, "material", as when an object belongs to someone.

In the eternal language of human love, however, "my" really shows reciprocity, the equal balance of the gift in true mutual personal communion. In this case, the nuptial meaning is preserved. In love's language, "my" is really a radical denial of the subject-object relationship. However, lust of the flesh removes this mutual belonging and "my" no longer has its heavenly meaning. This heavenly "my" does not include the "law of ownership" or "object of possession". It is concupiscence which is directed to these latter.

Enjoyment and Ownership

"Enjoyment" now means that the object has meaning for me and is at my disposal. The personal analogy of belonging opposes this meaning and shows that what comes "from the Father" is different than what comes "from the world". Concupiscence drives man to enjoyment and ownership. As a result, disinterested giving is excluded by selfish enjoyment.

The Opposition of Lust

Lust bears witness to the state of the human spirit (Jn.2:16). John's words show an opposition which is buried in the human heart between spirit and body. This effects the mutual relations of persons.

The "desire of the body" becomes more powerful than the "desire of the mind" because there is "another law at war with the law of my mind." (Rom.7:23). Christ's appeal to the human heart alerts us to this constant danger.   *July 30, 1980*

34. A HISTORY WRITTEN BY LUST

Hardness of Heart

In confronting the Pharisees about divorce Jesus said, "For your hardness of heart Moses allowed you to divorce your wives, but from the beginning it was not so." (Mt.19:8). The Old Testament sees "hardness of heart" causing the disruption of God's original plan. This helps us to interpret Israel's legislation on marriage.

Christ uses this phrase "hardness of heart" to confront the "inner person". Lust is a distortion of God's creation and Christ speaks His words to the man of lust. Jesus' words about "hardness of heart" proclaim the new ethics of the gospel which are deeply connected with "the beginning innocence". They are realistic and addressed to man as he is today, the man of lust.

To Every Man

Christ always knew "what is in every man" (Jn.2:25). His words about lust and "adultery in the heart" are a judgment upon every man. This is the ethical judgment of Christ's gospel. Although Christ spoke to men of His own culture, these words speak to every historical man, the man of lust. Christ speaks to the inner experience of every man in every place and in every age. His gospel speaks to every man. Every human heart is unique and defined by each person's inner humanity. Yet, Christ's words apply to all.

Lust in History

Lust conditions the inner being of every man. Human history is written under the pressure of this lust and historical ethics is connected with this lust. The force of lust decides human behavior and forms social structures and institutions. Because we always encounter this lust, no study of ethics can ignore this fact of the man of lust.

Therefore, we need a more detailed study of Christ's words about committing adultery "in the heart" (Mt.5:27-28).

August 6, 1980

35. JESUS REJECTS AN OLD TESTAMENT TRADITION

Interpreting the Sixth Commandment

When Jesus spoke of adultery, He was speaking to a Jewish audience who knew the Ten Commandments. They also knew that their prophets had reproved the people for breaking these commandments. Jesus' words confronted a human interpretation which did away with the correct meaning of the sixth commandment. Jesus wanted the justice of His disciples to be "superior to that of the scribes and Pharisees." This would be impossible unless He gave to the sixth commandment its correct interpretation.

Jesus, therefore, rejects the centuries-old interpretation, (which changed the law due to the varied weaknesses of the "man of lust"). This Old Testament casuistic interpretation was superimposed upon the original commandment's meaning. Christ wanted to recover the commandment's fundamental clarity because He came not "to abolish but to fulfill" the law and prophets (Mt.5:17). This fulfillment demanded a correct understanding.

Old Testament Practice – The Patriarchs

The Old Testament provides many examples which show how the sixth commandment was put into practice. First, there was a widespread defection from monogamy. In the time of the patriarchs (Abraham, Isaac and Jacob) this defection was dictated by a desire for offspring. Wives who were barren told their husbands to conceive by another woman so they could have children "on their own knees". Sarah said this to Abraham (Gen.16:2) and Rachel said this to Jacob (Gen.30:3). These stories show the moral atmosphere of Israel because the patriarchs exemplified the highest religious level.

After Moses

The sixth commandment was given to Moses after Abraham, Isaac and Jacob had died. However, the commandments did not change this tradition of how Israel acted. The patriarchs' motives for committing adultery was to have children. This motivation was greatly expanded by the kings of Israel, (David and Solomon), who were influenced by concupiscence and established polygamy in Israel's culture.

When David, who had taken other wives, committed adultery with Bathsheba the wife of his subject, Uriah the Hittite, (2Sam.11:2-27) he repented. In David's mind, "adultery" meant taking another man's wife. For David, adultery did not mean taking many wives. The Old Testament shows that monogamy, having just one wife, was never part of the Old Testament ethics from King David to Jesus.

Adultery – Narrowly Defined

Concerning this sixth commandment, Israel put all of its religious efforts into promulgating laws of divorce. The Old Testament took a determined stance against adultery, and even employed radical means (the death penalty) to enforce this stance. Adultery, however, was narrowly defined as the violation of the man's right of possessing his legal wife (usually one among many). This differs greatly from God's original plan which intended monogamy. While severely condemning adultery, Israel supported and fully legalized polygamy.

The Woman In Adultery

When Jesus faced the accusers of the woman caught in adultery, He did not refer to Israel's divorce laws when He spoke of "whoever is without sin". His hearers put down their stones because they recognized a wrong engraved in their human heart which was deeper than a legislated norm. When Christ said "Go, and sin no more." he clearly identified adultery as a sin (Jn.8:11).

Christ needed to correct this Old Testament history which distorted the norm contained in the words, "You shall not commit adultery." *August 13, 1980*

36. THE SIXTH COMMANDMENT – COMPROMISED BY ISRAEL'S TRADITION

Rejecting Israel's Legal System

The people who listened to Jesus knew this sixth commandment against adultery, but in Old Testament history, the Jewish people had distorted this command. As the legalizing of polygamy became more evident, the juridical aspects had to increase. This caused an increased number of precepts and severity for violations.

Jesus, in establishing the indissolubility of marriage, confronted this basic contradiction in Israel's legislative system, which allowed a man to have many wives, many concubines and cohabitation with slaves. In trying to curb abuses, the system actually protected the social dimension of adultery and caused

God's commandment to be misinterpreted. Therefore, Christ rejected the traditional legal system.

Failure of the System
The Old Testament clearly condemned sexual deviations, such as homosexuality, bestiality and Onanism (Gen.38:8-10). Its matrimonial law stressed the procreative purpose of marriage and, at times, tried to be just, saying that both the woman adulteress and her male companion should be put to death. (Usually, however, the woman was treated more severely.)

No Order in the Heart
By its laws, Israel made sexuality "objective" and confirmed the "shame" aspect of sexuality. Sex is seen as impure and the discovery of nudity is equivalent to the completed sexual act. This legislation shows that Israelite society evaluated sexual acts in a negative way.

In spite of this, the Old Testament did not destroy the teaching on original innocence and was not a forerunner of Manichaeism (which saw the body as evil). The Israelite legislation is not "negative" but rather "objective", trying to put Israelite sexual and social life in order. However, the law did not attempt to order the heart of man.

Also, a bond existed between morality, law and medicine. Certainly these laws contained many practical precepts regarding hygiene drawn from experience. In this vast sphere of human problems, medicine, law and theology should always be closely linked.

The Teaching of the Prophets
In trying to restore Israel's conscience, Christ rejected the traditional interpretations of what constituted "adultery". Besides social legislation, the Old Testament provided a tradition of the prophets who used the analogy of "adultery" to describe Israel's greatest sin, the abandoning of the true God for the false cults. Yahweh is a spouse united by nuptial love to Israel. By idolatry, Israel betrays her spouse just as an adulterous woman betrays her

husband. This analogy provided a relevant interpretation of adultery which was sorely needed in Israel's legislation.

Especially, Isaiah, Hosea, and Ezekiel show God's love and Israel's betrayal. Isaiah highlights the love of God who always takes the first step toward the unfaithful spouse. Hosea and Ezekiel clarify the ugliness and moral evil of unfaithful Israel. The next chapter penetrates these prophetic texts. *August 20, 1980*

37. THE PROPHETS SPEAK THE UNCOMPROMISED TRUTH

The Help of the Prophets

Christ wanted to restore the sixth commandment, "Thou shalt not commit adultery", which had been obscured by the Israelite legislation on marriage and sexual activity. The prophets helped to restore the commandment by saying that Israel's abandoning of God is "adultery".

Hosea

God commanded Hosea to marry a prostitute and have children by her (1:2). Although Israel is like the wife who "went after her lovers" (2:13), God always searches for Israel and awaits the day when He will again be called Israel's husband, saying "I will betroth you to me in righteousness" (2:16; 19-20). God threatens Israel to "make her as she was the day she was born" (2:4-5) if she is not faithful.

Ezekiel

Ezekiel, in a wider sphere, sees God caring for Israel from birth. When she was a little child "sweltering in blood", God helped her to grow to full maidenhood, clothed her, made a covenant with her, and clothed her with gold and silver. Israel, however, trusted in her beauty and played the harlot. She became an adulterous wife receiving "strangers instead of her husband" (16:5-32).

In this strong way, Ezekiel expresses the analogy between adultery and idolatry, both of which are betrayals of love. God is the generous "spouse-consort" Who receives numerous betrayals by Israel's cult of idols. In Ezekiel, God's choice of Israel is all one-sided, made by the husband at the time of his wife's birth, an act of pure mercy toward a helpless infant. This is a correct definition of God's covenant with Israel.

The Prophet's Meaning of Adultery

Most important, the prophets give adultery a meaning which differs greatly from Israel's legislation. For the prophets, adultery constituted a breakdown of a personal covenant. For the legal tradition, adultery was a violation of ownership, primarily the ownership of the woman by the man.

Israel's acceptance of polygamy did not alter the prophets' idea of adultery. For them, adultery was the antitheses of the nuptial relationship. Only a monogamous marriage accomplished the needed interpersonal alliance and constituted the union when "man ... cleaves to his wife and becomes one flesh" (Gen.2:24). Such bodily union is their bilateral "right" and a regular sign of their communion. Adultery, committed by either, violates this right and is a radical falsification of the sign. In contrast to Israel's legislation, the prophets express adultery very clearly.

Christ's Teaching

Adultery, a sin of the body, falsifies the interior truth of marriage. Christ established the exact reason for its sinfulness by comparing the moral evil of adultery with the moral goodness of marital faithfulness. The structure of marriage is governed by the inner communion of the two people, which corresponds to a covenant, whether of man-woman or of Yahweh-Israel. A true understanding of the marital covenant shows adultery is a violation of this pact.

"Adultery is a sin of the body", and is an act in which two people who are not husband and wife form "one body". The sin of the body is identified through the fact that the two people are not spouses. A true union of the body must be a true sign that the people are husband and wife. *August 27, 1980*

38. THE WISDOM BOOKS PRESERVE GOD'S TEACHING

Adultery in the Heart

Besides disputing with the lawyers or the moralists of the Torah, Christ openly rejected the legislation of Israel as the determining factor of morality. In this legislation, the interpersonal relationship of spouses was overshadowed and darkened by the objective relationship of <u>property</u>.

Christ went further and said that every man who looked with lust on a woman committed adultery (Mt.5:28). He counterpoised adultery in the heart with adultery in the body. Why does Christ shift adultery "to the heart" when adultery is in the body? Christ's words, "adultery in the heart" demand a deep understanding of man. They shift adultery from the body to the heart, which is the place of "desire".

The Man of Lust

In speaking of the man who "looks lustfully", Christ referred to the man of lust who, because of concupiscence, desired and looked lustfully. Christ spoke both of a human experience (psychological) and an aspect of salvation (theological). Theological and psychological must always pervade one another. This truth has great significance for Jesus' ethics, especially "looking lustfully".

The Wisdom Books

For Christ's immediate listeners, His words recalled the admonitions of the Wisdom books, (Proverbs, Sirach, and Ecclesiastes). These have a certain one-sidedness because the admonitions are addressed to men. Women, in these warnings, are seen as occasions of sin, or even as seducers. However, Proverbs and Sirach also praise the woman who is "the perfect companion of her own husband" (Pr.31:10) and who, as a good wife, makes her husband happy.

Frequent Admonitions

Sirach praises a wife in her well ordered home, who has a "beautiful face or a stately figure" and "whose charm delights her husband" (26:15-18). However, this praise contrasts with frequent admonitions when the beautiful woman is not the man's wife and is the cause of temptation or adultery, "Do not desire her beauty in your heart" (Pr.6:25). "Turn away your eyes from a shapely woman." and "Many have been misled by a woman's beauty." says Sirach (9:8-9).

No Change of Heart

These Wisdom texts protect the moral order, because they teach virtue which is based on God's law and human experience. They possess a knowledge of man, develop a moral psychology and come very close to Christ's call to the human heart. However, there is no evidence that these words changed Israelite ethics. These Wisdom books use human conscience to teach morals which the Book of Ecclesiastes synthesizes into a philosophy of human existence.

Although the warnings are clear, they do not transform the ethical situation of Israel. (Such a transformation had to wait until the Sermon on the Mount.) However, these wisdom books prepared Jesus' listeners to adequately understand adultery and that lustful look which constituted adultery in the heart.

September 3, 1980

39. SIRACH DESCRIBES LUST AND CONCUPISCENCE

Sexual Passion Described

Jesus' listeners were prepared by the Wisdom books to understand "adultery in the heart". Sirach speaks of man's fornication not ceasing until the fire (of passion) burns him up. It describes the adulterer as one who falsely believes that walls can hide his acts from God, when in reality, God can see the woman who gives birth to a stranger's child.

Although world literature contains descriptions of lust, Sirach contains the "classic" elements of carnal concupiscence in the comparison between concupiscence and fire. This fire invades the senses, excites the body, seizes the feelings and possesses the heart. It even suffocates the inner voice of the person's conscience.

External modesty in regard to others gives the appearance of decency but within the man of lust there is a fear of concupiscence and not a true fear of evil. By suffocating conscience, passion brings about a restlessness of the body, a restlessness of a man whose inner voice has been silenced. Passion, once released, has an insistent tendency to satisfy the senses (Sir.23:17-22).

No Peace

Although this gratification should satisfy the senses, it touches only the outermost level of the human person. The biblical author says that the man who is committed to sensual gratification finds neither peace nor himself. He is consumed and pays no attention to his inner conscience. Passion wears out and exhausts itself. Only when passion enters into the whole person, into the profound energies of the spirit, does it become a creative force and undergoes a radical transformation. If passion suppresses inner conscience, it wears out and man is consumed.

The Listeners Understood

Because Christ spoke to every man who understands lust from his own internal experience, He did not describe lust extensively as did Sirach (23:17-22). He merely called attention to lust, realizing that his listeners understood that lust is intrinsic to the heart and to conscience.

What A "Look" Reveals

Christ did not describe lust, but paused on the threshold. In His words, lust is not yet an exterior act of the body, but an interior act of the heart, "a look". Yet, a "look" can be understood and can reveal the person's concern. A "look" expresses what is within the heart. Christ says a man looks according to what he is within, and by a look, man reveals his interior state.

Christ says that a "look" is the threshold of an inner truth and He singles out a look of lust. Lust shows that the man places a false value upon the body. A man looking lustfully destroys the nuptial meaning of the body, which must be linked to the sacrament of matrimony, and is part of the self-giving in every relationship, (as will be shown later).

By His words on lust and "adultery in the heart" Christ taught that lust, like adultery, destroys the body's nuptial meaning, and is defined as "adultery in the heart".

September 10, 1980

40. LUST DESTROYS THE RICH VALUES OF MASCULINITY/FEMININITY

The Bible and Psychology

When a man looks lustfully at a woman, he experiences a conflict of conscience and of personal dignity.

This biblical meaning of lust differs from the purely psychological meaning which sees lust as an intense inclination toward an object because of its sexual value (a definition in most books). While not underestimating this definition, the Bible sees lust impairing an important ethical value. Lust deceives the human heart which should experience the body of the other as a call to a communion of persons.

The Mutual Attraction

This call is the perennial mutual attraction of masculine and feminine. This indirect invitation of the body to a relationship is not the lust condemned by Christ. True lust, the bearer of concupiscence, really diminishes this invitation and reciprocal attraction. The eternal feminine, as well as the eternal masculine, tend to free themselves from concupiscence and seek achievement in the world of people. Christ's words confirm this sphere of human striving which forms the mainstream of human culture.

Reduced by Lust

Lust reduces the original mutual attraction of masculinity/femininity, and closes down an important aspect of the horizon of human persons. A man who is conscious of the value of sex as part of the rich storehouse of feminine values is quite different from a man who reduces all feminine values to sex as a gratification. The eternal attraction to the feminine sets free in man a whole gamut of spiritual-corporal desires which correspond to a true value. Lust limits this gamut of desires and obscures these values.

Destroying the Meaning

Lust obscures the significance of the body and of the person. Femininity ceases to be for the man a language of the spirit, a sign of the wonderful matrimonial significance of her body. Lust ruins this matrimonial significance and aims only to satisfy the body's sexual needs.

According to Christ, this lust takes place in a "look", a purely interior act. A look is an act of knowledge, which becomes lustful when concupiscence enters. "To look at lustfully" means both an act of knowledge and an act which will arouse lust in the other. Lust is an appetite which seeks the object for its own satisfaction and Jesus' words highlight this interior intention for the other person.

When a man looks with lust, the woman ceases to be the object of eternal attraction and becomes the object of carnal attraction. *September 17, 1980*

41. LUST REDUCES PERSONS TO "OBJECTS"

The Effect of a "Look"

When a man looks lustfully at a woman she is deprived of her meaning as a person. Instead of being the "eternal feminine", she becomes only an object for man, a potential satisfaction of his sexual need. Although the act is interior, expressed only by a "look", a deep change occurs within the man due to his intention. Without this inner change, "already committing adultery in his heart" would have no meaning.

The Dynamism of Lustful Intentions

By this intention, a certain woman is not a subject of attraction for a personal relationship but is the object of the man's sexual need. When this happens, the man's heart is enslaved, and lust becomes a desire. This intention sweeps the will along and brings about a relationship to a woman according to the values of lust. When lust gains the will's possession it can be said that lust dominates the person. By lustful choices, the relationship toward the other is established and the lustful intention acquires its full power over the person.

From that subjective moment on, the description of Sirach (23:17-22) is confirmed about the man dominated by lust. There is a more or less complete compulsion of the body and the loss of the freedom of the gift.

As Objects For Each Other

Desire transforms the man and makes a certain woman the object of potential sexual satisfaction. We are not at all questioning the need for sexual satisfaction, but there is a question of the relationship of persons and the need for their mutual relationship to serve the unity of the communion.

Two persons can exist as objects for each other, satisfying each other's sexual needs. This reduces the richness of the reciprocal man/woman attraction and extinguishes the personal meaning of their unity. "A man ... cleaves to his wife, and they become one flesh" (Gen. 2:24) describes a mutual relationship. Lust destroys this relationship by pushing their personal union toward only the utilitarian goals of sexual satisfaction.

By recapturing the original human interior experience affirming the heart as this sphere of the inner man, Christ's words aim at transforming sexual ethics.   *September 24, 1980*

42. UNDERSTANDING "ADULTERY IN THE HEART"

Three Part Teaching

Jesus' teaching has three parts: First, "You have heard that it was said, 'You shall not commit adultery'". Second, "But I say to you that everyone who looks at a woman lustfully ..." Third, "... has already committed adultery in his heart." Christ lists three separate elements, namely, to commit adultery, to desire to commit adultery in the body and to commit adultery in the heart. Dividing the text into three parts is useful, as long as we see their relationship to each other.

Adultery

Concerning adultery, Jesus had to free the sixth commandment from the interpretations given by Old Testament practice, so that justice would abound. His new ethics are based upon values which had been lost.

Looking Lustfully

"Do not commit adultery" is a prohibition which excludes a given moral evil. The ninth commandment says, "Do not covet your neighbor's wife." Christ did not nullify this ninth commandment, but aimed at a deeper clarification of adultery. Please note that Jesus changes His style from normative to narrative and describes an interior fact, ("looking at a woman with lust"). This is easily understood. By describing this interior fact, Christ shows how the commandment must be understood and practiced.

Adultery in the Heart

The third part, "committing adultery in the heart", reveals the new essential values. A paradox emerges because Jesus speaks of committing adultery when no external act has taken place. It would seem that adultery can be committed only in the flesh, by two people who are not husband and wife. Is Christ just using a metaphor to highlight lust's sinfulness?

To admit this would be to identify adultery only with an exterior act of people who live together in a conjugal way, but who do not have a married status recognized by society. If so, then Christ's saying, "Everyone who looks at a woman lustfully" would be limited to the question of the person's status. On the contrary, Christ is talking about looking lustfully at any woman, not just another man's wife.

A husband cannot commit adultery in his heart with his wife because he cannot commit adultery with her in his body. She is his wife and he alone has the exclusive right to look lustfully at her. A husband's interior act of desire can never be called adultery.

The Richness of Christ's Teaching

Although the ninth commandment seems limited ("Do not covet your neighbor's wife.") we have already seen the richness of Christ's words about "in the beginning" (Mt. 19:8) and, therefore, we must seek a deeper understanding of His words, "adultery in the heart". These words show an awareness of both human sinfulness and of the body's redemption.

Christ criticized the one sided interpretation of adultery derived from the Old Testament failure to observe monogamy. He also made "adultery in the heart" independent of the man and woman's juridical status of being married. His moral evaluation is based in the dignity of the persons, whether unmarried or married.

October 1, 1980

43. FREEING RELATIONSHIPS FROM THE POWER OF LUST

A Wider Meaning

"Lust in the eyes" is defined by Christ as "adultery committed in the heart". The ninth commandment gives this "inner lust" a restrictive meaning, namely sexual desires for another man's wife. Christ's words have a wider meaning and refer to every woman. Therefore, we need to amplify and deepen this interpretation. When Christ speaks of a man "looking lustfully", He did not say the woman was necessarily married. He focuses, not on the state of the woman, but on the dignity of man and of woman.

Utilitarian Satisfaction

Lust of the flesh is a permanent element of man's sinful, lapsed nature. This lust, springing from inner sinfulness, makes the woman exist "for" the man and reduces the richness of the masculine/feminine to a satisfaction of man's sexual needs, (something akin to the animal instinct). The woman is reduced to an object and the mutual "for" each other is destroyed by the utilitarian goal. The woman, in her femininity is chosen to satisfy the man's instinct. Even a husband can commit this adultery in his heart if he treats his wife as only an object for his sexual instincts.

62

Although psychology interprets lust as the satisfying of an instinct, this meaning is far too shallow to grasp Christ's thought. The theological interpretation is much clearer, because it links the lustful act with man's permanent sinful disposition.

Inner Purity Needed

Jesus remained faithful to the Old Testament because He saw that the inner recesses of the human heart had to be revealed. The command to avoid external acts, "Do not commit adultery", demands a human heart which is interiorly pure. Jesus even speaks of "plucking out one's eye" and "cutting off one's hand" if these cause sin (Mt.5: 29-30). The severe external legislation of the Old Testament did not stop adultery because the law's interpretation was compromised by the lust of the flesh. Only a consistent firmness against this lust of the flesh can insure purity of heart.

Conflict With Marital Unity

The reason not to commit adultery is based upon the indissolubility of marriage. Adultery conflicts with marital unity which is based on the dignity of the person. Christ strengthens marriage when he attacks "adultery in the heart", seeking man's full liberation from inner lust. Cleansed of lust's constraint upon the human spirit, the couple can truly be mutually "for each other", enjoying full interior freedom. Only with this personal freedom can any marriage be lived in truth.

Relationships Free From Lust

Christ's teaching forces the listeners to seek what has been lost by sin, namely the fullness of the mutual relationship. Besides the indissolubility of marriage, Christ envisioned that every form of relationship between man and woman (which constitutes the very fabric of society) would be free from lust. All human life is "coeducative" and everything depends on "who she will be for him and he for her".

We must not fear the severity of the words spoken by Christ who knew what is in man's heart and yet brought about "the redemption of the body". October 8, 1980

44. ANSWERING TWO IMPORTANT QUESTIONS
A TRUE ETHICS

The Two Questions

Christ's reference to the heart throws light on those inner desires of man which arise from lust. Every "historical" man, even if he does not know Christ, questions his own heart. "Is the heart doomed to evil or is it called to good?" A second, more practical question is, "How must the historical man act who accepts Christ's words?"

Our teaching helps with these questions. The question, "How can he act?" forces man to look at his inner self. The question, "How should he act?" reveals the ethics, the moral behavior which commits historical man to definite patterns of thinking and feeling.

Ethical Norms and Practice

These two questions have been answered in an infinite number of ways. From among this multitude of responses, we must isolate the true ones that flow from man's conscience and his moral sensitivity. In this way, practice will interpenetrate ethics and true behavior will result. Ethical norms are worked out by moralists, but real ethical answers are given by living men. They are the subjects of real morality and co-authors of morality's history. On this level rests either the progress or decadence of morality. Christ, in his Sermon on the Mount, spoke to such men.

Christ and Human Ethics

Christ's words are powerful because they are so concise, especially when compared with all that is written in secular literature. The history of human ethics flows in many streams, with individual currents sometimes coming close to one another and then moving further away. In judging his own body, historical man goes from pessimism to optimism, from puritanical severity to modern permissiveness. This must be kept in mind, so that Jesus' words maintain their clarity concerning human actions.

False Interpretations of Christ's Words

How have Christ's words echoed in the human history of ethics? An echo transforms both the original voice and words and is sometimes full of mysterious fascination. With Christ, the opposite has happened. His words have been stripped of simplicity and depth. They have been given meanings which are far from His true meaning. Some interpretations even contradict His original meaning. For example, the history of Manichaeism (which arose in the East from Mazdeistic dualism) saw matter as the source of evil which was manifested in man mainly by sex. For them, Jesus' condemnation was extended to marriage and conjugal life.

The severity of this heretical system might seem in harmony with Christ's words to "pluck our your eye" or "to cut off your hand". A purely material interpretation of Christ's words about "adultery in the heart" could lead to a Manichean interpretation. This heresy claims that evil is concealed and manifested in the body. In truth, Christ's words do not condemn the body but place a demand on the human spirit.

Other teachers use Christ's words as a "loophole" to avoid the demands of the Gospel. Really, His words are an affirmation of the body, an affirmation of masculinity and femininity, and of the personal aspects of "being a body".   *October 15, 1980*

45. SEEING THE FULL VALUE OF SEX

Not a Condemnation

Christ's words do not contain a condemnation nor an accusation of the body, but rather a condemnation of the human heart, specifically, the heart of a man of lust. Even here, Christ doesn't accuse, but subjects that heart to a judgment, a self-critical examination, "Does your heart succumb to the lust of the flesh?" Christ's judgment about desire affirms that the body is an element which, together with man's spirit, determines man's subjective being and shares in his personal dignity. Christ's judgment on lust has a meaning essentially different from Manichaeism.

"From the Beginning"

The body is meant to manifest the human spirit. When Christ spoke of a man leaving his parents and cleaving to his wife, He defended the inviolable rights of marital unity. His teaching has nothing in common with Manichaeism. When speaking of our waiting for "the redemption of the body" (Rom. 8:23), Paul does not say that the body is evil but that man is sinful and has forgotten the clear nuptial meaning of the body.

Sex – An Under-Appreciated Value

The body is a manifestation of the spirit and Christ defended conjugal unity as a sacramental sign. Christ's words must be totally free from any Manichean interpretation, which would negate the value of human sex or, at best, would tolerate sex for the necessity of procreation.

Christian ethics transforms man's attitudes so that every person can realize the Creator's original plan. Human sex is at the service of the communion of persons, the deepest level of human ethics. For Manichaeism, sexuality is an anti-value. For Christianity, sexuality is an under-appreciated value. Seeing the value of the body allows for the historical redemption of the body. Christianity says that "human nature is both fallen and redeemed".

An Accusation Which Invites

Christ's words confront the "complex truth about man". By His accusation He invites man to overcome the evil, to detach himself from inner lust, and not to see the body as evil. Accepting the Manichean view that sexuality is an "anti-value", would be no victory over lust and would conceal the danger of justifying inner lust. Christ never taught that the object of lust, the woman who is looked at, is evil (a clarification which is sometimes lacking in Wisdom books of the Old Testament).

The Full Value of Sexuality

Christ's words ask us to discover the true value of the human body because this value is not sufficiently appreciated. He wants us to discover the full value of sexuality. "Adultery in the heart" is a devaluation, an impoverishment, and a deprivation of the value of the woman. The Manichean view of the body is totally alien to Christ, who invites us to rediscover the dignity of the body and the dignity of sex.   *October 22, 1980*

46. CHRIST OVERCOMES THE "THREE MASTERS OF SUSPICION"

Three Masters of Suspicion
Christ's words call us to overcome the three forms of lust, especially lust of the flesh. The modern problem comes primarily from the contemporary teachings of Freud, Marx and Nietzsche. Recoeur described these teachers as "masters of suspicion", because suspicion is the foundation of their systems of thought. These three thinkers converge with Christ's gospel in their judging and accusing man's heart, and they might seem to judge the heart according to John's three forms of lust.

The Three Judgments
Nietzshe's judgment and accusation corresponds to John's "lust of the eyes". Marx's interpretation corresponds to the "pride of life" and Freud's interpretation corresponds to "lust of the flesh". We, too, (like these three thinkers) could have placed the human heart in a state of "continual suspicion". However, in condemning lust, Christ does not allow this lust to be the absolute criterion of human ethics. Truly, lust is important in understanding man's actions, but lust is not the absolute criterion of man or of ethics. Therefore, the psychological interpretation of lust is not enough. If man combats these forms of lust by human nature alone, he cannot overcome their influence.

Christ Versus Freud
Christ's words differ from the Freud's. He does not allow us to stop at the accusation of the human heart and to continually see that heart "with suspicion". His words are an "appeal to the heart" and He moves us to the "redemption of the body" (Rom. 8:23). Man's heart must not be filled with irreversible suspicion because of lust and the libido, which is so stressed by

psychoanalysis. By redemption, man is effectively called to rediscover the body's nuptial meaning and his interior freedom. This comes from a mastery of lust.

The Invitation
Christ's words call man "from the outside", and also "from the inside". If historical man allows Christ's words to have power over him, he will be able to hear a true echo of the call "from the beginning". Christ appealed to this "beginning" to remind man and woman that they exist for each other.

The Power and Call of Redemption
Christ's words are not hurled into the emptiness. He does not speak to a man completely absorbed in lust who cannot even imagine the true mutual relations of man and woman. Christ says that the original power of creation can become for historical man the power of redemption, and can touch his deepest level. Even while experiencing lust, man also feels the opposite attraction. He experiences the need to preserve the dignity of mutual relations imbedded in the masculine and feminine body and to fill these relations with all that is noble and beautiful, conferring on them the supreme value of love.

Christ's words invite us to rediscover the whole meaning of human life and conjugal love. Christ's teaching is the antithesis of Freud and the antithesis "of suspicion". His words reveal not just another ethics, but another vision of man's possibilities. Man is not "irrevocably accused" by his lust, but is irrevocably called to love. Christ's words reveal man's true heritage, much deeper than his heritage of the three forms of lust. *November 5, 1980*

47. THE BEAUTY OF THE EROTIC
(RIGHTLY UNDERSTOOD)

Eros and Ethos
Although Christ's words accuse the human heart, they are primarily an appeal. Let us bring this discussion closer to the teaching of contemporary men by a discussion of "Eros". "Eros" is a Greek term brought from mythology into philosophy and then

into literature and finally into spoken language. "Eros", unlike "ethos" is not part of the biblical language. "Eros" has one meaning in philosophy and a different meaning in literature. In truth, "Eros" has a vast range of meanings, and there is a need to evaluate these meanings.

In contrast, "Ethos" has a clear meaning. As used in philosophy and theology, it deals with good and evil. By Ethos, the human will makes choices which are subject to the laws of conscience and to the sensitivity of the human heart.

Plato's Definition
"Eros", according to Plato, is the interior force which brings man toward all that is good, true and beautiful. This attraction leads to an intensive, subjective act of the human spirit. This definition certainly contrasts with modern literature's focus on the sensual attraction which draws man and woman to seek the unity of the body. Because Genesis speaks of this conjugal union, we must ask if "Eros" connotes the same meaning. Also, because of the modern meaning given to "Eros", we must understand clearly how Christ speaks of lust.

The False Common Understanding
Common language usually limits "Eros" to a sensualistic attraction. Scientific research, in limiting "Eros" to this meaning, faces a danger of reducing sexual attraction to the physical. This common usage stresses the subjective straining toward an object because of its sexual values, which exert a powerful attraction upon man's psyche. "Looking at a woman lustfully", and external behavior flowing from lust, are considered "erotic". This reasoning equates the erotic with the acts flowing from lust and would mean that Christ expressed a negative judgment on the erotic and a severe warning against "Eros".

Many Shades of Meaning
However, "Eros" has many shades of meaning. The mutual actions by which man and woman approach each other and unite in one body are erotic. To understand what Christ said about the "erotic", we must consider the various shades of meaning.

Certainly, Christ did not condemn "Eros" as defined by Plato. In fact, knowing the many definitions of "Eros" helps to understand the complex riches of the human heart to which Christ appealed.

No Condemnation

Christ does not condemn "Eros", seen as an interior force attracting man to all that is true, good and beautiful. Christ's ethos of redemption shows the necessity of overcoming all lust, and reveals the possibility of transforming the man of lust. "Eros", as an attraction to all that is true, good and beautiful, is not opposed to ethos, (the norms of behavior). They both meet in the human heart.

Ethos, with its commandments and prohibitions, seems to have a negative view of the erotic and Christ's words could be seen as a prohibition in the erotic sphere. Really, Christ's words try to protect the essential values of the erotic, making them accessible to the human heart. *November 5, 1980*

48. SAFEGUARDING THE DEEP INNER RICHNESS OF THE PERSON

The True Gift in the Erotic

Christ's ethos reveals a new order of values which demands that we rediscover the true gift contained in the erotic. If the human spirit does not do this task, then the body's passions will stop at mere lust. If the body stops at lust, man will never experience the fullness of Eros and the erotic will never seek the true, good and beautiful. Eros desperately needs ethos.

Without ethos, spontaneity cannot flourish in man's erotic life. Many erroneously believe that ethical norms of behavior hinder the erotic, and that the erotic needs to be freed from these moral norms. Because this opinion has repercussions in behavior, it hinders a true discovery of the full dimensions of Eros.

Power of Christ's Words

Everyone accepting Christ's words must realize that they are called to that full and mature spontaneity which comes from the perennial attraction and which is a gradual fruit of discerning one's own heart.

Great Demands
Christ's words are severe, demanding a deep consciousness of one's own interior acts, an awareness of internal impulses and an ability to maturely distinguish them. Christ demands that the sphere of body and sex, seemingly man's exterior sphere, be controlled by the interior man. This happens only by obeying correct conscience and mastering inner impulses. Man must guard this inner spring and draw purity of heart from all his varied impulses. Only in this way, can he gain the inner space of freedom.

A Complete, Inner Evaluation
By his consistent perseverance, man must learn the meaning of masculinity and femininity, not only abstractly but in his own concrete interior reactions. This is a "science", a deep knowledge of human interiority by which a man learns to distinguish what comes from God's creative attraction and what comes from lust. Because these various inner movements can be confused with one another, Christ calls the interior man to a mature and complete evaluation of the inner movements of his heart. This is a task worthy of man.

Needed For Spontaneity
Because man has a deep inner richness, he needs to distinguish his inner impulses in order to enjoy true human spontaneity. Noble gratification differs from sexual desire. Sexual desire, when linked to noble gratification, differs from simple desire. Sexual excitement differs from the deep emotions of a person's response to the masculine and feminine. Christ's words are severe because they contain deep requirements concerning human spontaneity.

Enjoying Spontaneity

The man of lust who is devoid of choice and of a hierarchy of values, does not have this spontaneity. It can only be gained by self-control. By mastering his instincts, man rediscovers the spiritual beauty of the human body. Guided by a true conscience, the person enjoys a spontaneity which the carnal man cannot even imagine. Christ's words lead to a spontaneity of interior acts. They free man's noble aspirations by linking the erotic with the ethical. *November 12, 1980*

49. THE NEW MAN – REDEEMED AND SET FREE

Christ's Newness – The Redemption of the Body

Christ's words are both ethical and human, connecting moral norms with historical man. Christ gives to the interior man a moral code which is new in comparison with the Old Testament and in regard to the state of historical man. After original sin, historical man became the man of lust. Christ's newness is universal, independent of history and geography.

The Ethos of Redemption

We call Christ's teaching "the ethos of the redemption of the body", following St. Paul who calls lust "bondage to decay" and "submission to futility" (Rom.8:20-21). Paul contrasts lust with the desire for "the redemption of our bodies" (8:23). "All of creation groans" and "waits with eager longing to be set free and obtain the glorious liberty of the children of God" (8:20-21). St. Paul reveals both man's lustful situation after sin and man's aspiration for a redemption of his body.

The Revealing Teachings

Christ reveals the fullness of this redemption when He speaks of the resurrection of the body (Mt.22:30; Mk.12:25 and Lk.20: 35-36). His words about "adultery in the heart" also speak of this redemption of the body. Although Christ's context is the Old Testament law and prophets, He primarily refers these questions to "the beginning", the mystery of God's original plan of creation.

72

The Ethos of Redemption and of Creations

Christ did not invite man to return to "original innocence" (which is irrevocably lost) but to rediscover how man, now redeemed, can live. Christ forges a link between creation and redemption. The ethos of redemption requires us to recall the ethos of creation. By confirming the commandment, "You shall not commit adultery", Christ leads man to·a new view of his heart and then to a new way of being and acting. In the new man, the redemption of the body dominates the lust of the flesh. Temperance and mastery of desires form the interior man. Obviously, the ethos of redemption demands self-control, immediate continence and habitual temperance in every area.

Not Self-Emptiness

Temperance and continence do not mean an emptiness of values nor an emptiness within the person. Self-mastery, the control of desires, binds the person to true values which lust would destroy. By acts of mastery, the person obtains a deeper power and firmness concerning the perennial attraction of man/woman which the Creator has written in their hearts.

Experiencing Dignity of Person

Certainly, there is an "emptiness of the subject" when the person must decide for the first time to attain self-mastery (or when a habit of lust has been formed). However, even in this first time of self-mastery (and even more as the capacity for continence increases) the person experiences his own dignity.

By temperance, he protects what is personal in him, and experiences his freedom to respond adequately to the body's nuptial meaning. As self-mastery is achieved, the deepest layers of the inner person acquire a voice which lust would never permit to be heard. These layers cannot emerge when there is the permanent suspicion of the human heart (as taught by Freud) or when the Manichean anti-value of the body is dominant.

Reciprocating the Original Call

Christ's words are a call and not an accusation. To acquire purity of heart, man must be conscious of human sinfulness. This ethos of redemption is rooted in the realism which sees the sinful state of man. The unique and unrepeatable man decides from his heart, (the symbol of human choice). Christ's call to purity of heart recaptures the moment when man was called from his original solitude and liberated by his openness to the woman, because purity of heart always refers to the other person, who is "co-called".

December 3, 1980

50. LEADING TO A LIFE ACCORDING TO THE SPIRIT

What Comes From Within

In the Sermon on the Mount, Christ expressed what is opposed to purity, "looking lustfully at a woman", and demanded purity. "Blessed are the pure of heart, for they shall see God" (Mt.5:8). Man's inner self is the source either of purity or impurity.

Christ said that what goes into a man's mouth does not defile him. Man is defiled by what comes out of his mouth, that is, from his heart (Mt.15:11). "For out of the heart comes evil thoughts, murder, adultery, fornication, theft, false witness and slander. These are what defile a man ..." (Mt.15:18-20; also Mk.7:20-23). "Purity" or "pure" contrasts with "dirty" or "polluted", as a dirty room or polluted air. A filthy body must be washed to remove dirt.

Wrong Emphasis

The Old Testament gave great importance to the physical washing of hands and had detailed instructions of bodily ablutions to remove sexual impurity (Lev. C.15). These seemed to be hygienic regulations which later acquired religious meaning and became ritual cleansings. Because of these "ritual cleansings" the Old Testament developed an erroneous understanding of moral purity. Christ radically opposed this understanding and said that absolutely nothing from the outside makes a man interiorly impure and no external ablution can produce moral purity. Purity must come from the heart.

Christ carefully did not connect moral purity with bodily washings. Sexual "dirtiness", in the bodily sense, is not part of His moral definition of purity or impurity (Mt.15:18-20).

Purity As A General Concept

In a sense, all moral evil is compared to "uncleanness". Christ's words dealt with many sins, "evil thoughts, murders, adultery, fornication, theft, false witness and slander". Therefore, moral "purity" or "impurity" is a general concept. All moral good is a purity and all moral evil is an impurity.

Because Christ's words (Mt.15:18-20) are not just connected with the sixth and ninth commandments, His phrase "the pure in heart" refers both to the general and the specific meaning of purity. St. Paul, at times, uses "purity" in the wider sense, and at times, he uses it in the limited sense, meaning "sexual purity". Christ's words "looking with lust at a woman" directly speak of this sexual sphere.

John and Paul

While St. John (1Jn.2:16-17) contrasts what comes "from the Father" and what comes "from the world", namely the threefold lust of "flesh, eyes and the pride of life", St. Paul writes of the tension between "flesh" and the "Spirit" (meaning the Holy Spirit) in Galatians (5:16-17). For Paul, life "according to the flesh" is in opposition to life "according to the Spirit". "For those who live according to the flesh set their minds on the things of the flesh, but those who live according to the Spirit, set their minds on the things of the Spirit" (Rom.8:5). The next section begins this new theme - that purity is realized by a life according to the Spirit.

December 10, 1980

Part Three
St. Paul's Teaching on the Human Body

51. LIFE "ACCORDING TO THE FLESH" OR "ACCORDING TO THE SPIRIT"

"Of the Flesh" and "Of the World"

St. Paul highlights the tension within man. "The desires of the flesh are against the Spirit, and the desires of the Spirit are against the flesh" (Gal.5:17). These are not two essential elements of body (matter) and spirit (soul). Paul presupposes that this disposition of forces was formed in historical man by original sin. Now, the body opposes and easily prevails over the spirit.

Paul's words coincide with John's three-fold lust. "Flesh" for Paul means both the "exterior" man and the man "interiorly" subjected to the world. He is clothed in those values that belong to the world and which the world imposes on him. Both Paul and John speak of secularism or sensualism. The man living according to the flesh seeks only what is of the world. He is a man of the senses and of the threefold lust.

Flesh and Spirit – Opposite Poles

The man of flesh lives at almost the opposite pole of the Spirit, Who wants a reality different from the flesh. The flesh prevents "you from doing what you would" (Gal.5:17). Paul even writes of doing evil which he didn't want to do. He speaks of the impossibility, or limited possibility, of doing the good that he wants (Rom.7:19). The tension between flesh and spirit is manifested as an inner fight between good and evil. Although Christ speaks of an interior act, Paul calls it a "manifestation of the flesh" and shows how life according to the flesh opposes life according to the Spirit. Because of inherited sin, life in the Spirit is exposed to and succumbs to life according to the flesh.

Diverse Goals

Paul says that those who live according to the flesh set their minds on the goals of the flesh. This is death because the flesh is hostile to God. It does not and cannot obey God. Those in the flesh cannot please God.

Those who live according to the Spirit have the goals of the Spirit. These are life and peace. When the Spirit of God dwells within, the body is dead but the spirit is alive (Rom.8:5-11).

Anticipating Justification

Paul also goes back to "the beginning", when sin brought about "a life according to the flesh". However, he also anticipates the victory of Christ's resurrection. This justification in Christ is intended for every historical man and is given to the interior man. This justification is a real power which is revealed in man's actions.

Diverse Results

Paul describes the works of the flesh, as "fornication, impurity, licentiousness, idolatry, sorcery, enmity, strife, jealousy, anger, selfishness, dissension, party spirit, envy, drunkenness, carousing and the like" (Gal.5:22-23). He lists the fruits of the Spirit, "love, joy, peace, patience, kindness, goodness, faithfulness, gentleness and self-control" (5:22-23).

Ethos of Redemption

Therefore, the interior power of "life according to the flesh" and "life according to the Spirit" bring forth diverse actions. Paul's man "of the flesh" is John's "man of lust". The man "of the Spirit" manifests the ethos of redemption. This ethos brings about a dominion over the three-fold lust, and refutes the accusations and the suspicions of the human heart.

The "ethos of redemption" brings forth the fruits of the Spirit. By each virtue, the human spirit is permeated by the Spirit of God. It deliberately chooses good and overcomes the desires resulting from the three-fold lust. This self-control is not "man's works" but "fruits of the Spirit".   *December 17, 1980*

77

52. THE SPIRIT FREES US FROM THE POWER OF THE FLESH

Faith in Christ's Redemption

When Paul speaks of the contrast between life according to the flesh and life according to the Spirit, he expresses deep faith in an ethical realism of Christ's redemption of the body. Although this redemption has cosmic significance, man is the focus. Within man, the Spirit brings forth the justice sought by Christ.

Works of the Flesh – Opposed to the Holy Spirit

When Paul lists the "works of the flesh" (Gal. 5:19-21), he mentions sensual sins (fornication, impurity, licentiousness) and other sins (idolatry, sorcery, enmity, strife, jealousy, anger, selfishness, dissension, party spirit, envy). These latter are not usually seen as carnal or sensual. They are sins which correspond to John's "lust of the eyes" or "the pride of life". In describing all these sins as "works of the flesh", Paul uses "flesh" in a wider meaning, not opposed so much to man's spirit but to the Holy Spirit.

Paul's "works of the flesh" correspond to Christ's words (Mt.15:2-20) about the sins which come from within a man's heart (such as "theft, false witness and slander"). Both Paul and Christ use the word "impurity" in the wider sense, referring to all sins from within (as well as the specific sins of sexual impurity). For Paul, the "works of the flesh" are all those actions opposed to the work of the Holy Spirit.

Putting to Death the Deeds of the Flesh

Paul reminds the Romans that we are not "debtors to the flesh" because "living by the flesh" will cause our death. By the Holy Spirit, we put to death the "deeds of the flesh" so we might live (8:12-13). Paul's words "body" and "Spirit" have a richness of meaning. Putting to death the deeds of the body by the help of the Spirit is exactly what Christ spoke about. This self-mastery, the "putting the works of the body to death" is the indispensable condition for life in the Spirit, because "life according to the flesh" inevitably results in the "death" of the spirit.

Heaven

Paul, in Romans and Galatians, constantly widens this horizon of "sin-death" by speaking often of heaven. Paul writes, "Those who do such things shall not inherit the kingdom of God" (Gal.5:21). This also applies to "the fornicator, the impure man, or one who is covetous" (that is, an idolater) (Eph.5:5). These works that exclude from the kingdom extend to all kinds of sins, although sins of sexual impurity are at the top the list (cf Eph.5:3-7).

Set Us Free

For Paul, the Holy Spirit is manifested in behavior marked by freedom, for Christ "has set us free" (Gal.5:1). We are "called to freedom" which must not be used as "an opportunity for the flesh" but to be "servants of one another" (Gal.5:13-14).

For Paul, justification is carried out in and through Christ. It is not achieved by carrying out individual prescriptions of the law, especially circumcision. In this way, Paul frees his listeners from a carnal concept of justification. For Paul, redemption comes "from the Spirit" and not "from the flesh". We must realize that by gospel purity Christ has "set us free".   *January 7, 1981*

53. A FREEDOM ACCORDING TO THE LAW (GAL. C.5)

Free to Love and Serve

Paul's freedom is an opportunity to serve others, not to serve the flesh, (Gal.5:13-14). This highlights the opposition between "body-spirit", an essential point in Gospel ethics. Notice that Christ sums up the Old Testament law in the two commandments of charity, (of God and neighbor). His new gospel appeals to human freedom for the full potential of the human spirit.

Paul does not say freedom does away with the law, but that freedom is subject to the law of love. The vocation to be "free in Christ" means choosing life "according to the Spirit". Realizing the danger in freedom, Paul writes clearly that freedom is not "an opportunity for the flesh" (Gal.5:13).

The False Freedom

Paul foresees that the "bad use" of freedom opposes a true liberation of the human spirit. Christ's freedom leads to service and to new works "of the Spirit". Using freedom as "an opportunity for the flesh" is a negation, a pretext, and a false freedom.

This false freedom is really John's threefold lust. As the person submits to this lust, he becomes incapable of true freedom and is no longer a gift for another. Paul echoes Christ and sees that gospel purity is linked to all the virtues which are at the service of charity.

Comparing the Works of the Flesh and of the Spirit

The "works of the flesh" are whatever is morally bad. The "works of the Spirit" are whatever is morally good. In listing the "works of the flesh", Paul puts fornication, impurity and licentiousness in first place (Gal.5:19). However, he does not list "purity" among the "works of the Spirit", but names only "self-control", (which means continence in all the sensual areas, especially the sexual).

Self-control is opposed to fornication, impurity and licentiousness, as well as to the sins of drunkenness and carousing. Although purity is the correct way of acting in the sexual sphere, it receives only an indirect mention by being included in the virtue of "self-control". Because Paul contrasts the sexual "works of the flesh" with the "works of the Spirit", purity is obviously one of these "new works".

A More Direct Teaching

Paul speaks more directly when he asks the believers at Thessalonica to "abstain from unchastity: that each one of you know how to control his own body". This must be done "in holiness and honor, not in the passion of lust like heathens who do not know God" (4:3-5). Paul writes that "God has not called us for uncleanness, but in holiness" (4:7-8). The next chapter shows how purity contributes to man's holiness.   *January 14, 1981*

54. HONORING THE BODY (FIRST THESSOLONIANS)

Purity As Control

In First Thessalonians, Paul defines purity as a man knowing "how to control his own body in holiness and honor, not in the passion of lust" (4:5). Each word deserves an adequate comment.

Purity is a capacity to abstain from unchastity because the pure man knows "how to control his own body". This practical capacity allows a man to act in a given way and to avoid acting in the opposite way. This capacity is rooted in the person's conscious choices. St. Thomas Aquinas says that sensitive desires ("appetitus concupiscibilis"), must be mastered and subordinated. Purity consists in containing the impulses of these sensitive desires which focus on the sensual man.

Control "In Holiness"

Although Paul teaches that purity is the controlling of sensual desires, he speaks positively. Purity's main task is not abstention but "control over one's own body in holiness".

Abstaining and controlling depend on each other. Controlling one's body is impossible without abstaining. This overcoming of the sexual attraction bestows meaning and honor upon these sexual instincts which arise spontaneously and have repercussions in man's affective-emotional sphere. As such, they must be integrated into the personal order.

"In Honor"

Control of one's body "in holiness and honor" is not just a capacity of man. It is a work of the Spirit who makes this human capacity a fruit of "honor". Self control is an "honor" for man and for the other person, male or female. This "honor", the essential power to control the body in holiness, is a power of the Spirit. He gives man an inner capacity to act justly, even when man experiences the multiple impulses of lust, and sometimes even surrenders to them.

Paul's View of the Human Body

In First Corinthians, Paul will formulate his view of the human body, "God arranged the organs in the body, each of them, as he chose." (12:18). He goes on, "On the contrary, the parts of the body which are weaker are indispensable, and those parts of the body which we think less honorable we invest with greater honor, and our unpresentable parts are treated with greater modesty, which our more presentable parts do not require." (12:33) He writes that God arranged the organs of the body. To those parts considered less honorable we give greater honor, covering them with greater modesty. So God gives greater honor to the inferior parts so there is no discord and the members care for one another (1Cor.12:22-25).

In the next chapter, we will study this text which deepens our theology of the body.   *January 28, 1981*

55. PAUL DESCRIBES THE BODY – THE "HONORABLE" AND "LESS HONORABLE" PARTS

A Christian Evaluation

In First Corinthians (12:22-25), Paul gives a realistic description and a Christian evaluation of the human body. A scientific description of the body is inadequate for our purposes. The body is used by a person to express himself, and the body must be evaluated as an instrument of the person. This is the perennial theme of culture, literature, sculpture, painting, dancing and the theater (a theme worth dealing with separately).

Paul's description, although not scientific or biological, is certainly real. He evaluates the body in light of the mysteries of the creation and the redemption of the body. His spiritual attitude of respect for the holiness of the body springs from creation and redemption. He has neither the Manichean contempt for the body nor any naturalistic cult of the body.

As "In the beginning"

The human body is permeated by the dignity of the human person. Although it is a body conceived in sin, it retains the experience of original innocence. Paul's words, "the unpresentable parts", "the weaker ones" and the "less honorable" describe the shame which was experienced after sin. Although this shame is now within man as the fruit of lust, it carries an echo of original innocence. It is the negative impression which was left behind by the loss of a positive value.

Man's Response to Shame

The body has "unpresentable parts", not because of their physical nature but because man, in his shame, sees them as "unpresentable". However, due to "shame" man invests these "less honorable parts with greater honor" and treats "the unpresentable parts with greater modesty" (1Cor.12:23). Shame brings about greater respect for the body. This respect corresponds to the Creator's plan, "God has so composed the body".

Experiencing Discord

Paul writes that we "honor the inferior parts so that there may be no discord in the body". This discord shows the state of man after original sin. The man of original innocence, male and female, felt no discord in the body. They "were naked and not ashamed" (Gen.2:25). In original creation, God gave the body a harmony and the mutual care of the members. This harmony allowed man and the woman to experience the unifying power of their bodies, the basis of their personal communion.

Discord – The Reason For Shame

In First Corinthians (12:18-25), Paul says that historical man experiences shame due to "discord in the body", and has a need for modesty. The path to victory, to overcome this state of discord, is "to control one's own body in holiness and honor". By using the expressions "less honorable" and "weaker parts" Paul highlights the "honor" which he mentioned in First Thessalonians (3:4), especially in the sphere of behavior towards one's own body and in relations with others.   *February 4, 1981*

56.   THE HOLINESS OF THE TEMPLE
(THE HUMAN BODY)

The Spirit's Work

In First Corinthians, Paul highlights the respect due to the human body and the need for purity to detach the body from the power of lust.   Purity safeguards the dignity of the person in relation to their masculinity or femininity.   This new capacity which comes from the Holy Spirit.   Paul connects the moral virtue (man's work) with the Spirit's gift when he calls the body "a temple of the Holy Spirit".

A Profanation of the Temple

"Do you not know that your body is a temple of the Holy Spirit within you, which you have from God?   You are not your own."(6:19).   Previously, Paul had been severe, "Shun immorality. Every other sin which a man commits is outside the body, but the immoral man sins against his own body." (6:18).   Therefore, impurity is a sin "against the body", and opposes the virtue by which man keeps his body "in holiness and honor" (1Th.4:3-5).

Sexual sins do not just profane the body, depriving it of honor. They are also a "profanation of the temple," because now the human body has a two-fold dignity.   The first is due to the human spirit, and the second is due to the Holy Spirit Who dwells within.   Man's body is no longer his own.   It is the body of a human person and a temple of the Spirit.

Bought By Christ

By redemption, the body has received a new dignity, (union with Christ, the Person of the Word).   Man has a new obligation because he has been "bought with a price" (1Cor.6:70).   The believer must awaken to the duties of this new and double gift.   No one must sin "against one's own body" (1Cor.16:18) because "the body is not meant for immorality but for the Lord, and the Lord for the body" (1Cor.6:13).

In Jesus Christ, every human body is elevated into the supernatural realm.   Every Christian must consider his behavior towards his own body and the body of others.   In light of the new

84

measure of holiness in the body. We must control our bodies "in holiness and honor" (1Th.4:3-5).

To Whom United?

Paul stigmatizes unchastity, "Do you not know that your bodies are members of Christ? Shall I therefore take the members of Christ and make them members of a prostitute? Never! Do you not know that he who joins himself to a prostitute becomes one body with her?" In contrast, "He who is united to the Lord becomes one spirit with him." (1Cor.6:15-17). This mystery of redemption began when the Word became flesh and now bears fruit in every believer, especially by the fruit of ethical purity.

Being "bought with a price" (1Cor.6:20) demands a special commitment to control one's body in holiness and to abstain from unchastity. *February 11, 1981*

57. PIETY – A REVERENCE FOR THE SPIRIT'S TEMPLE

Piety – A Sensitive Reverence

When Paul calls the body a "temple of the Holy Spirit" and reminds Christians that they are "members of Christ", he teaches that we have a special moral duty to "control our bodies in holiness and honor".

Redemption includes the seven gifts of the Spirit (Isaiah 11:2), one of which, "piety", is especially helpful to purity. Piety, reverence for God, makes the human person sensitive to the dignity of the human body because it is a temple of the Spirit.

Controlling one's body leads to a deeper experience of God's love imprinted within man. Paul writes "So glorify God in your body" (1Cor.6:20). Purity, together with piety, brings a fullness to the body's dignity and glorifies God. Purity is the glory of the human body before God and is God's glory in the body. From purity springs a beauty in man's common life, making personal trust possible.

Purity and Wisdom

Paul's teaching on purity shows a continuity with the Wisdom books. "Remove from me evil desire, let neither gluttony nor lust overcome me" (Sir.13:4-6) and "I directed my soul to him (Wisdom) and through purification I found him" (Sir.51:26). These texts show that purity is a condition for wisdom and wisdom is a condition for purity. Purity prepares for wisdom and wisdom strengthens purity.

Jesus taught that the "pure of heart" (man's virtue) would "see God" (the gift of the Spirit). Paul shows the full dimensions of purity in this life, "To the pure, all things are pure". He describes the problems caused by impurity "to the corrupt and unbelieving nothing is pure" (Ti.1:15).

Here "to be pure" refers to all morality and specifically to sexual morality. Paul's idea of purity as" life in the Spirit" has its roots in the redemption of the body, expressed ultimately in the resurrection. In a later section, we will see how Jesus connected purity with the resurrection of the body.

58. A REVIEW OF JESUS' TEACHING ON "LOOKING LUSTFULLY"

A Review of the Teaching

Jesus' words that "looking at a woman lustfully" constituted "adultery committed in the heart" (Mt.5:27-28) required a deep reflection. This is also true of His words that "from the beginning" God had made them "male and female" and "What God has joined together, let not man put asunder."(Mt.19:3-6).

We have reflected on man's original innocence and the truth that the image of God is stamped upon the mystery of the person, who is male and female. Based on this truth, Christ taught the indissolubility of marriage. This truth of man being male and female must also be studied in the light of man's hereditary sinfulness. Christ's words clarify the threefold lust in man.

The Wisdom Literature

Jesus defined "looking with lust" as "adultery committed in the heart" because his immediate listeners understood these words in the tradition of the Old Testament prophets and the Wisdom literature. Although modern man perceives these words from a diversity of cultural backgrounds, Christ always speaks to every generation.

Purity of Heart

The truth, "You shall not commit adultery" is an ethical norm. Christ shows that the lust of the flesh must be overcome. In truth, the "purity of heart" taught by Christ means freedom from every kind of sin. However, we use the phrase "purity of heart", to mean sexual purity. According to Paul, purity comes from the Spirit. By urging his listeners to avoid lust and to acquire purity he shows those values which the human heart must pursue.

Original Innocence

Christ's words show an ethical truth which is essential for every man. By recalling how it was "in the beginning", Christ places the man of original innocence within the mind of historical man.

Christ is realistic and does not direct man backward to an original innocence which is forever lost. He points forward to a purity which frees the man of lust. This purity comes from the Holy Spirit through the power of the Redemption of the body. By opening himself to the Spirit, man can rediscover the value of his body.

Purity's Positive Meaning

By purity, a man does not just abstain from unchastity but discovers the dignity of the body (1Thes. 4:3). By purity, the full truth of the body is revealed. The body is a means of full personal communion between man and woman. For the man of lust, purity seems to have negative function. However, Christ and Paul show the positive function of purity. There is victory over lust and the manifestation of the Spirit's power in His temple, the body. Piety restores a simplicity to the body in its man/woman relationships and creates a spiritual climate which is very different from "the passion of lust". Satisfying passions is quite different from the joy of a self-mastery which allows the person to be a gift for the other.

April 1, 1981

59. THE COUNCIL AND POPE PAUL VI SPEAK

A Teaching for All Peoples

Christ's words concerning lust and "adultery committed in the heart" (Mt.5:27-28) refer to all peoples, because they appeal to the human heart. This history of good and evil is also a history of the salvation which is explained in the gospel. The power of the Holy Spirit is given to whomever believes in that gospel.

The theology of the body is a teaching which gives requirements and which motivates men to fulfill Christ's command. Christ's teaching on the indissolubility of marriage and the overcoming of lust show that the Creator has assigned to men and women the task of interpersonal communion in which the persons make an authentic gift of themselves. This teaching leads to a full education of man.

Biological Teaching

Medicine, which describes the body's functioning as an organism, does not develop man's awareness of the body as a sign of the person and a temple of the Spirit.

This development of biological science has provided one-sided knowledge. Using this one-sided approach, the body is treated as an object of manipulation. This approach deprives the body of the dignity which is proper to the person. Many questions demand a full view of man for correct answers. Biological knowledge helps in discovering the body as a free gift for others only if the person is spiritually mature. Otherwise, this knowledge has the opposite effect.

Theology of the Body

The theology of the body provides this teaching. It sees the male and female body as a task given to the human spirit. By spiritual maturity, the person realizes that the body becomes a sign of the person and authentic "matter" in the communion of persons. Lust dims and obscures this meaning.

Two Documents

From this theology of the body we can understand two important Church documents, "The Dignity of Marriage and the Family" from the Vatican II document "The Church in the Modern Word" (Part 2, Chapter 1) and Pope Paul VI's encyclical on birth control (Humanae Vitae). Because Christ's words on the dignity of marriage converge with these two documents, they will be the theme of the book's final section.

Disfiguring the Beauty of Marriage

The Council documents say that polygamy, divorce, free love and other disfigurements obscure the excellence of marriage. Also, married love is profaned by selfishness, the worship of pleasure and illicit acts against human generation (GS #47). Pope Paul writes that he is alarmed by the growing use of contraceptive methods which forgets reverence for the woman, disregards her physical and emotional equilibrium, reduces her to an object of satisfaction and no longer sees her as man's partner (H.V. #17). Both Christ and St. Paul had the same concerns.

Periodic Continence

Pope Paul states that the mastery of instincts demands a self-control, especially regarding periodic continence. This control will not hurt conjugal life but will give it a higher human value. Although demanding continual effort, periodic continence helps the spouses to develop their personalities, to enrich each other, to give attention to the other and to remove selfishness (H.V. #21).

The theology of the body helps us understand Pope Paul's encyclical. The purpose of this theology is to "insure" that the "affective manifestations" which are "proper to conjugal life" conform to the moral order and the dignity of the person. As Pope Paul says, we need "to create an atmosphere favorable to education in chastity" (H.V. #22).   *April 8, 1981*

A full understanding of Pope Paul's encyclical (Humanae Vitae) is given in the book's final section.

Part Four
Ethical Norms for Modern Communications

60. THE ETHICAL QUESTION OF THE HUMAN BODY IN WORKS OF ART

Objective and Subjective Experiences
In the theology of the body, we have often focused on the aspect of personal subjectivity. The body is not an objective reality remaining outside of man's personal consciousness. The problems of the body are really problems of the person and are closely connected with the person's experiences of his/her body and experiences of relationships. Paul's words to "control our bodies in holiness and honor" show both the objective and subjective dimensions.

The Body in Works of Art
Works of art enable the body to extend outside a living person. Through works of art people experience the body. This is usually an aesthetic experience (from the Greek meaning "I look. I observe"). In art, the body exists outside of the living person according to the artist's activity.

The Viewer
However, the one who views the work of art is deeply bound to the original model. The contemplation of the artistic work cannot be totally detached from the experience and reactions of seeing the person who modeled the work. This experience cannot be isolated in the person's conscience from Christ's warning about lust. Therefore aesthetic experiences are also subject to the ethos of the body, which necessitates a climate favorable to purity.

Ethical Questions in Works of Art
This climate can be endangered by the objective reproduction of the body in works of culture, in social communications which use the spoken or written word and in the reproduction of images, both traditional and modern, (as in

sculpture, drama, ballet modern audio-visual techniques). Obviously, many ethical questions arise concerning the human body as an object of culture.

Important Distinctions

The human body is the perennial object of culture because man is the subject of culture and he involves his body. Although works of art are an "objectivization" of the body, some distinctions must be made. First, there is the human body in the theater, in ballet, or in a concert. Second, there is the human body in painting and in sculpture. Third, there is the human body in a quite different category. This arises when the human body is put into films or in photographs.

In sculpture and painting, the human body is a model undergoing specific elaboration by the artist. In film and photography, the model is not transfigured by the artist. The living man is reproduced and the human body becomes an object of reproduction.

"Objective Reproduction"

This distinction is essential. By reproduction on television or in film, the human body becomes an anonymous object, whether an anonymous photograph in an illustrated magazine or an image diffused on the movie screens. This anonymity results from its "propagation", objectivized by the technique of reproduction. This differs from the body of the model which is transfigured by the artist. The anonymity of the film and of television hides the person who is reproduced. This is a specific moral problem, especially in the mass media.

We need, therefore, to extend Christ's words about "looking with lust" and "adultery in the heart" to the whole world of art so we can create "an atmosphere favorable to chastity".

April 15, 1981

61. PORNOVISION AND PORNOGRAPHY –
OBJECTIVIZING THE HUMAN BODY

Christ's Questions to the Artistic Culture

The ethos of the body are those ethical norms that govern the body's nakedness because of the dignity of the person. This ethos has a nuptial system. The personal relationship of the parties must be appropriate and adequate so that they can be naked before each other, as a reciprocal gift to each other. Obviously, such an ethos of the human body, called by Christ "as it was in the beginning", raises moral questions in works of the artistic culture.

Taking Possession

The artistic objectivization of the naked human body, male and female, loses its subjective meaning and is no longer a gift to another specific person. The viewers take possession of the body. This "taking possession" already happened when the artist transfigured the living model into his work of art.

Obviously, a very delicate problem arises here, which very much depends upon the motives of the artist and of the viewers. Although problems arise, this does not mean that the human body, in its nakedness, cannot become the subject of art. It does mean that these works of art are not morally neutral.

Covering Due to Shame

We spoke previously of "shame". The couple, in their original innocence, "were both naked and were not ashamed" (Gen.2:25). However, after sin, they experienced a personal shame which necessitated a privacy. The man and woman covered their own bodies.

This covering of the body is necessary to guarantee that the body is a true gift to each other. Culture shows a specific tendency to cover the nakedness of the body, and this "covering" shows a growth in man's personal sensitivity. This "covering" contrasts greatly with the anonymous nakedness of the body in the mass media. By clothes, a culture shows a sensitivity to the dignity of the human person. (Some cultures allow nakedness but this is due to the warmth of their climate.)

For A "Specific Other"

The body is meant to be a gift directed toward a specific other person in the man/woman relationship. Human cultures, even in this state of sinfulness, show an explicit understanding that the body is meant for a specific other. The feeling of "shame" preserves the body for that special other. The person with developed sensitivity has a strong sense of shame which is set aside only in the proper setting.

Certain situations, such as medical examinations, necessitate the undressing of the body. An opposite example is important. In concentration camps, nakedness was imposed to destroy personal sensitivity. A man, sensitive to the dignity of the body, does not wish to become an object through anonymous nakedness, nor does he want another person to be an object for himself.

Pornovision and Pornography

However, due to his threefold lust, man can be incited to act contrary to this belief. In these cases, lust is felt in the individual person and in the whole state of social morals. This happens in the visual reproductions of nakedness in the mass culture, when the reproduction of human nakedness (in film or television) becomes "pornovision", or in written literature when it becomes "pornography".

Acting Contrary to Shame

Both occur when the limit of shame is overstepped, when personal sensitivity to human nakedness is disregarded and when the right to the privacy of the body is violated. In these cases, the ethical norms that the human body should be a mutual gift between specific persons are set aside. These rules of shame, inscribed and incised within the person, require the human body to fulfill its call to an interpersonal communion.

Observing these norms is important in creating a climate favorable to chastity.

April 22, 1981

62. MEDIA REPRODUCTION DESTROYS THE PERSONAL GIFT

Violating Personal Sensitivity

Christ's warning about "looking with lust" must be extended to the artistic culture, especially the visual mass media, which has such an impact upon modern man. Both "pornovision" and "pornography" violate personal sensitivity toward the human body. The right to the privacy of the body in its masculinity and femininity is violated.

Obviously, this violation of the human body as a mutual gift to a specific person can be violated in the intention of those who do the artistic reproduction. Shame and personal sensitivity are violated when the naked body, as a model, becomes part of social communication. What is meant to be private becomes "public property".

The Full Realism

Representatives of "naturalism" protest these ethical norms, saying that there is a right to "everything that is human". They claim that there is a "realistic truth about man". Really, they fail to consider the "whole truth about man" namely, that the privacy of the body is connected with the body's masculinity and femininity, a mystery inscribed deep within the person. This is the full realism of man.

The human body is a manifestation of the person, a sign of trust and of giving to another human person. The person who receives this gift, must respond in an equally personal way. The body, in its nakedness, is an element in human inter-personal communication. Because the body has such great value in this personal communion, making the naked body an object of reproduction is an ethical problem.

"Unknown Reception and Unknown Response"

By mass reproduction, the body as gift "enters an area of unknown reception and unknown response" becoming an "anonymous object" and an "object of abuse". The integral truth of man (what is personal and interior to him) establishes precise limits which must be accepted by the artist. No artist has the right to invite other people (the viewers) to contemplate images which violate these limits of personal sensitivity. In "pornovision" and "pornography" the naked body which should have deep value to another specific person (a giving of person to person), is uprooted from this personal communion and, by mass media, becomes an anonymous object.

A Condemnation For Eloquence

Condemning "pornovision and pornography" does not come from a puritanical mentality or a narrow moralism. This condemnation comes from the very eloquence of the human body which speaks of the value of personal dignity. Although these values can be reproduced in works of art, they can also be distorted and destroyed by the artist and by the viewers. We return again to Christ's words about "looking with lust" and "committing adultery in the heart". We must face these difficulties to create a culture which is favorable to chastity. *April 29, 1981*

63. IN WORKS OF ART – WHO HAS THE RESPONSIBILITY TO THE MORAL NORM?

Some Vital Questions

Christ's words concerning "looking with lust" and "adultery in the heart" (Mt.5:28) refer also to culture, especially to artistic reproductions of the naked human body. What is the relationship between the norms of the image (of verbal description) and the norms of viewing those images (or reading those descriptions)?

To what extent can the naked human body be the subject of a work of art and a subject of the social communication of these works? These questions are vital. In the audiovisual arts, the human body is connected with an "objective anonymity" which brings a serious threat to the true meaning of the body as a personal gift to each other.

Three Terms

The terms "pornography" and "pornovision" appeared relatively late in our culture. The ancient term is "obscene", (a Latin word) which indicates "everything that should not appear before the eyes of spectators". The "obscene" must be surrounded with due discretion, and should not be shown to persons without their own choice.

The Full Truth

Throughout the ages, the human body has been the model of works of art. Also, love between man and woman, and the full physical expression of that love, has been the subject of literary narratives. This is true even in the Bible, (especially in the Song of Songs). In literature and art, this important subject raises a question of the dignity of man in his masculinity and femininity.

The Artist and the Viewer

Although the artist certainly has a right, he also has an ethical responsibility to know the full truth of man and the full scale of values. The artist must have a purity of heart which guides his intentions as he creates his artistic reproduction.

Although "materializing" the model, he must also express his creative idea, the manifestation of his own interior values. In this way, he creates a unique transfiguration of the model. (We have pointed out before that an extremely important difference exists between art/sculpture and photograph/film.) The viewer, invited by the artist to look at his work, communicates not just with the "materialized" body but with the truth which the artist has succeeded in expressing.

A Hidden Sublimation or Technical Reproduction?

From antiquity, especially from Greek classical art, the naked human body has been the subject of art. Contemplating these works, the viewer can see the "suprasensual" beauty of the masculine and feminine body. These works hold within themselves an element of sublimation which leads a viewer to the personal mystery of man. They do not draw us into "looking lustfully" but to "purity of heart".

However, other works, especially in the field of visual reproduction, do offend human sensitivity because of the way the body is reproduced or portrayed. In the ethical consideration, these various factors of reproduction are decisive, especially when the reproduction is more technical than artistic (as photograph/film instead of art/sculpture).

Because of the art or media reproduction, the human body becomes accessible to the viewer. If our personal sensitivity responds with disapproval, it is because these works reduce the human body to the level of an object, an object of enjoyment intended to satisfy the lust of the flesh. This violates true artistic activity and happens especially in film and television.

"Ethos of the Image" and "Ethos of Seeing"

Pope Paul emphasized "the need to create an atmosphere favorable to the education of chastity" in which we live according to the dignity of the human body. Culture must affirm everything which ennobles human life. Sculpture and painting expresses man visually in one way; the play or ballet, in another way; and the film and television, in still another. Even literary works intend to arouse images.

This "ethos of the image" must be considered together with the "ethos of seeing" because creating an atmosphere of chastity involves both elements. The artist has ethical obligations in his creation of the image and the viewer has similar obligations.

True artistic activity chooses to overcome the anonymity of the body which would make it obscene (forced upon and not chosen by the viewer). The viewer must seek the "truth" expressed by the artist and not exploit the image by being a "consumer of impressions", staying only at the level of sensuality.

May 6, 1981

Part Five
Christ's Teaching on the Resurrection of the Body

64. THE FULL SURPRISE OF THE RESURRECTION

Third Series of Texts

Christ's words on the resurrection of the body are of fundamental importance to understand both Christian marriage and the renouncing of conjugal life for the sake of God's Kingdom.

These are the third series of texts which are constitutive for the theology of the body. First, Jesus spoke of human life "in the beginning" before original sin (Mt.19:3-9 and Mk.10: 2-12). Second, He warned about "looking with lust" and "adultery in the heart" (Mt.5:27-32). In this third text, Jesus reveals a completely new dimension of the mystery of man.

The Question of the Sadducees

The complex case laws of the Old Testament drove the Pharisees to confront Jesus about the indissolubility of marriage (Matthew 19 and Mark 10). On another occasion, the Sadducees, (who did not believe in the resurrection from the dead) confronted Jesus about the "levirate law", that is, a man must marry the wife of his brother who has died without conceiving any children. From this conversation, (reported in three gospels in almost identical fashion), there is a great revelation about the resurrected body. (Mt.22:24-30; Mk.12: 18-27; Lk.20:27-40)

The Sadducees were those "who say there is no resurrection" (Mt.22:23). Their argument is based upon a supposition of seven brothers, one of whom married a wife and died without children. Being faithful to the levirate law, the other six also marry her and die without any children. The Sadducees' question to Jesus is, "In the resurrection, whose wife will she be? For the seven had her as wife?" (Mk.12:20-23).

Ignorance of Scripture and of God's Power

Christ's reply points to the wisdom and power of God. He says, "Is not this why you are wrong, that you know neither the Scriptures nor the power of God? For when they rise from the dead, they neither marry nor are given in marriage, but are like angels in heaven" (Mk.12:24-25).

Examining the Important Texts

Knowing that the Sadducees wanted to disprove the resurrection of the body, Jesus said, "As for the dead being raised, have you not read in the book of Moses, in the passage about the bush, how God said to him, 'I am the God of Abraham, the God of Isaac and the God of Jacob?' He is not a God of the dead, but of the living" (Mk. 12:26-27). Twice in this passage (12:24 and 12:27) Jesus said, "You are wrong."

Luke introduces some elements not mentioned in Matthew or Mark. "Jesus said to them, 'The sons of this age marry and are given in marriage. But those who are accounted worthy to attain to that age and to the resurrection from the dead neither marry nor are given in marriage, for they cannot die anymore, because they are equal to angels and are sons of God, being sons of the resurrection'" (Lk.20:34-36).

Regarding the possibility of resurrection, all three gospels, refer to Moses (Ex.3:2-6). Moses had heard from the bush which "was burning, yet not consumed" the following words, "I am the God of your father, the God of Abraham, the God of Isaac, and the God of Jacob" (3:6). He also heard God's name, "I am who am" (3:14).

Therefore, in speaking of the future resurrection, Christ referred to the power of God.   *November 11, 1981*

65.   ABRAHAM, ISAAC AND JACOB – THE LIVING PATRIARCHS

Two Essential Elements

Matthew and Mark agree almost completely and contain two essential elements, the future resurrection of the body and the state of the body of the risen man. This enunciation is accompanied by Christ's words that the Sadducees "know neither the scriptures nor the power of God". These words define the foundation of faith in the resurrection.

Not Knowing the Scriptures or God's Power

The Sadducees treated the question of resurrection as a theory or an hypothesis. Jesus pointed out their "error of method" in not knowing the scriptures, and their "error of substance" in not accepting what was revealed. They did not know the power of God which was revealed to Moses at the burning bush. Jesus told the Sadducees, who were biblical experts, that literal knowledge of the scriptures is not enough. They forgot that the Bible exists so people can "know the power of God".

The Living Patriarchs

God revealed Himself to Moses as the "God of Abraham, of Isaac and of Jacob". When Christ spoke, these three patriarchs had been dead for a long time. However, Christ adds that God "is not the God of the dead, but of the living". Christ's interpretation of these words forces the hearer to accept the reality of a life which death did not end. Although according to human criteria all three were dead, Abraham, Isaac, and Jacob were still "living persons", ("for to him all are alive" Lk.20:38). Reading these words with faith shows that God is not bound by the law of death which rules man's earthly history.

Before Christ's Resurrection

Soon, Christ would give the final answer to this question by His own resurrection. However, for now, Christ limits His arguments to the Old Testament, seeking to know the power of God revealed in these words. These words about Abraham, Isaac and Jacob show that the living God gives life to those who live "for him". They have life even though they have been dead for a long time.

An Interpretation of the Teaching

This teaching means the following. He who is – Who lives and is life – is the inexhaustible source of existence as revealed "in the beginning". Due to sin, physical death has become man's lot (Gen.3:19) and man has been forbidden access to the tree of life. By His covenant with Abraham, Moses and Israel, God renews the reality of life, and, in a certain sense, again opens access to the tree of life. This life is given to those who had broken the original covenant by sin, had lost access to the tree of life, and, in their history, had actually died.

Fully Revealed in Christ

Christ is God's ultimate word on the subject. Through Him, God's covenant opens an infinite perspective of life. Access to the tree of life is now revealed to every man. This is the meaning of Christ's death and resurrection.

However, this conversation with the Sadducees takes place before Easter and contains no references to Christ's own future resurrection (which He had prophesied to His disciples). The reasons for this are clear. The Sadducees "say that there is no resurrection", and yet considered themselves biblical experts. That is why Jesus used Old Testament texts to show that they did "not know the power of God".

Jesus taught a God who gave life. The Sadducees deprived God of this life-giving power. Their God was no longer the God of the living but the God of their own interpretation.

November 18, 1981

66. A TRANSFORMED MALE AND FEMALE

Describing the Risen Body

After telling the Sadducees that God's power can bring about bodily resurrection, Jesus somewhat describes that risen body. "When they rise from the dead, they neither marry nor are given in marriage" (Mk.12:25).

After human beings have reacquired their bodies, in the fullness of their masculinity and femininity, they "neither marry nor are given in marriage". Luke prefixes this heavenly truth with the reminder about earth. "The children of this age marry and are given in marriage." (Lk.20:34)

Only to Earth

Marriage, a union characteristic of man from the beginning (Gen.2:24), belongs only to earth. It is not part of heaven because after the resurrection, marriage and procreation lose their purpose. Heaven is the definitive fulfillment of mankind, the quantitative closing of the number of beings multiplied on earth by the "conjugal unity in the body". Heaven is the world of God, Who will become "everything to everyone" (1Cor.15:28).

A Completely New State of Life
"That age", heaven, will be mankind's eternal homeland. It is the Father's house (Jn.14:2) which emerges from this present world in which the body is subjected to death. Christ teaches that the human person will reacquire his body and this union of body and soul will be a completely new state of human life itself.

After Christ rose from the dead, (a preview of man's own bodily resurrection) these words become a convincing promise. At present, we must study these words as understood before Jesus' resurrection. Christ reveals this new condition of man's risen body by comparing it with the body as it was "from the beginning".

Still Male and Female
"They neither marry nor are given in marriage" affirms that the risen bodies will be male and female. However, "being male and female" will be different than "from the beginning". Leaving father and mother, cleaving to a wife and becoming one flesh (Gen.2:24) shows the earthly relationship of man with woman, which is procreative.

Beyond Original Innocence
Luke's words (20:27-40) say that the risen human person "cannot die any more because they are equal to the angels and are sons of God". Man's body will undergo a spiritualization far beyond the state of original innocence. Yet, man will not be transformed into angelic beings. He will have his body.

Subject to the Spirit
Resurrection restores real life to the human body which was subject to death. The Bible always compares man with angels, and in the resurrection, man's similarity becomes even greater. Even though he will still be in his body, a new system of spiritual forces

will be released within man who will experience a new submission of his body to the Holy Spirit.

The resurrection is key in any theological study of man. Reflecting on the resurrection, St. Thomas Aquinas set aside Plato's idea of the body/soul relationship and drew closer to Aristotle. The resurrection shows that the body is not the "prison" of the soul (as Plato taught), but that the body and soul have a unity (as Aristotle taught). St. Thomas, in accepting Aristotle, saw that man's perfect happiness is not attained by his soul alone, but demands a union of the soul with the body.   *December 2, 1981*

67. THE DEFINITIVE VICTORY AT THE END OF HISTORY

A Perfect Inner System

Christ teaches about the spiritualization of man in the coming age. There will be a perfect system of inner forces between the spiritual and the physical. In contrast, historical man experiences multiple imperfections in his inner forces, seeing in his members "another law at war with the law of my mind" (Rom.7:23).

After the resurrection, man will be free from this inner opposition. "Spiritualization" means a full permeation of the body by the spirit, and of the body's energies by the energies of the spirit.

Perfect Participation in the Spirit

On earth, the body is subordinated to the spirit only by persevering work (even when the person is spiritually mature). On earth the possibility always exists of opposition between body and spirit. The resurrection removes this possibility and an essentially different state of the body results.

The person is not "dehumanized" but experiences perfect realization. There is a deep harmony between body and spirit and "perfect spontaneity" arising from the primacy of the spirit. This will not be a "definitive victory" of the spirit over the body, but the perfect participation of man's physical nature in his spiritual nature, the perfect personal realization.

Permeated by the Divine Presence

The "sons of the resurrection" are also "sons of God". This shows a divinization of man's humanity. Man's spiritualization will have its source in a divinization which is far superior to any state here on earth. The human being will be permeated by the divine and will arrive at a fullness which was totally inaccessible on earth.

This will be accomplished by grace, God's gift of His divinity to the full human person, body and soul. God will not communicate His divinity just to the soul but to the entire being. Man will enter into the fullness of communion with the three Divine Persons. This intimacy will not destroy man's subjectivity but will fulfill his being to an incomparable extent.

A New Meaning For the Body

In this divinization, the human spirit will experience love and truth in ways unknown on earth, ways in which the body also will share. "Neither marry nor are given in marriage" affirms the end of human history (so closely connected with marriage and procreation) and affirms a new meaning for the body. Do they teach the nuptial meaning of the body? To answer that, we need to understand the Beatific Vision, man's seeing God face to face, an experience beyond man's possibilities here on earth.

Seeing God – The Beatific Vision

The Beatific Vision is the self-communication of God to the whole of creation and, in particular, to man, who bears God's special image. In the Beatific Vision, man will see the mystery of the entire content of human history, a mystery hidden in the Father, revealed through Christ and accomplished by the Holy Spirit. Eternal life is the full experience of grace which man shared by faith on earth and which he experiences as an exhilarating reality in heaven.

December 9, 1981

68. "NOT MARRYING" –
THE TOTAL RESPONSE TO SEEING GOD

Not Marrying – Man's Perfect Reciprocal Gift

The heavenly union of man with God will be nourished by each person seeing God face-to-face. This is a share in the perfect communion of the Father, Son and Holy Spirit. As each person participates in this "other world" of perfect union with God, they will have their own authentic subjectivity and a perfectly mature subjectivity.

The Only Worthy Response

In this "other world" persons will be masculine and feminine in their risen body but they "will neither marry nor be given in marriage". Not marrying is the only adequate response to participating in the communion of Divine Persons because the Beatific Vision is a far greater gift than any earthly experience.

Not marrying is man's perfect reciprocal gift. All his energies and subjectivity are given to God. This virginal state of the body is the only response worthy of God. Heaven will be the complete fulfillment of the body's nuptial meaning. In heaven, the depth of love and consecration will totally absorb all man's subjective powers.

Discovering Perfect Communion With Everyone Else

In his total concentration upon God, man will rediscover himself and the union which he has to other persons. In his knowing and loving God, man will realize the mutual communion of all created persons. The two Catholic truths of a "communion of saints" and a "resurrection from the dead" are organically connected.

Christ's words about "not marrying" reveal that everyone will discover a new, perfect subjectivity and inter-subjectivity. The complete concentration upon God Himself will not take away the definitive fulfillment of the body's nuptial meaning. Heavenly reality will introduce man into a perfect realization of his sharing in God's communion of three Persons.

Three Stages of the Body

Christ's words (confirmed by His own resurrection) complete the revelation of the body in which historical man shares. By His words Christ takes us back, (before the beginning of sinful man) and also forward (into the life beyond death). These two extensions are not beyond a theology of the body because earthly experiences of man are still linked to "the beginning" and to "the age to come".

Man, then, has three stages of existence, his existence before sin, his historical experience, and his heavenly dimension. The consistency of man's image in these three stages contributes to the theology of the body.   *December 16, 1981*

69. THE HUMAN BODY – FULLY REVEALED IN GLORY

The Limitations of Reason

Rational methods can never reach these truths about these other two stages of man, "in the beginning" and "when they rise from the dead". Yet, carnal man carries these two other stages in his body, and the heavenly dimension becomes very important at the time of death. Christ's words about the future resurrection provide an image of man's new existence in a "future world" for which earthly life provides a base.

Connecting All Three Stages

The connection between life "in the beginning" and man's present life helps us to see the human body at the resurrection. In the beginning, God made them "male and female" (Gen.1:27), with the purpose that "they become one flesh" (2:24) in order "to increase and multiply" (1:29). "In the resurrection they neither marry nor are given in marriage", describes the development of another truth about man.

First, he has the same identity as in earthly existence. Secondly, although not marrying, he will still be male and female, as in the beginning. Therefore, in the mystery of man, created and redeemed, the meaning of male and female will exist outside of marriage and procreation.

Marriage – Just One Meaning of "male and female"

In his original solitude, man realizes he is a person who is meant for a communion of persons, the nuptial meaning of his body. However, marriage and procreation do not definitively determine the original meaning of male and female, but merely provide one concrete reality of the communion of persons in human history. "When they rise from the dead" indicates the end of that history. "Not to marry or give in marriage", although seemingly a negative definition, actually reveals a greater future state. This will be both personal and a perfect communion with others.

The Body's Completion in Glory

By his glorified body, man, male and female, will enjoy the face-to-face vision of God and will experience a completely new meaning of his body. This is not alienated from the other two experiences (the beginning and the historical). In this future state, man will experience the completion of what was already within him, potentially and historically.

The Full Revelation of the Body

The glorification of the body will reveal the definitive value of the body as a sign of the created person and a means of mutual communication. The perennial meaning of the human body, which struggles and suffers on earth, will be revealed again. In the glorified body all will have that freedom which will nourish a full communion in the great communion of saints.

Constructing an adequate image of this future world based only upon earthly experiences is difficult. However, we can approximate this future reality, by believing in the resurrection from the dead, eternal life, and the communion of saints.

A New Threshold

Christ's words help us to grasp this meaning of the body which is revealed throughout the Bible. From the beginning, God made them male and female so they could be "one flesh", a unity directed to eternal life. Genesis reveals the threshold of the theology of the body. "Not marrying or giving in marriage" present a <u>new</u> <u>threshold</u> which we must dwell upon even more.

January 13, 1982

70. PAUL'S DESCRIPTION OF THE GLORIFIED BODY (1COR.15: 42-46)

Paul's Experience of Christ's Own Resurrection

When Jesus engaged in polemics with the Sadducees, He never referred to His own resurrection but spoke of a God who is a God "not of the dead but of the living" (Mk.12:27). By the time Paul wrote his first letter to the Corinthians, Jesus had risen from the dead, and had appeared to many, including Paul himself. Therefore, Paul, in his controversies, could speak of the reality of Jesus' resurrection. "If Christ has not been raised, then our preaching is in vain and your faith is in vain ... But, in fact, Christ has been raised from the dead" (1Cor.15:24,20).

God's Reply to Historical Death

Christ's resurrection is the final self-revelation of the living God and the fullest confirmation of all revelation. In raising Jesus from the dead, God replied to the historical inevitability of death (which entered history when the covenant was broken). First Corinthians (C.15) shows the resurrection as the beginning fulfillment. In Christ, everything will return to God, "that God may be everything to everyone" (15:28). This is the definitive victory over sin when death itself will be destroyed (15:26).

Paul's Synthesis

Paul's synthesis is contained in the words, "What is sown is perishable; what is raised is imperishable. It is sown in dishonor; it is raised in glory. It is sown in weakness; it is raised in power. It is sown in a physical body; it is raised a spiritual body. If there is a physical body; there is also a spiritual body. Thus it is written, "The first man Adam became a living being; the last Adam became a life-giving spirit." (1Cor.15:42-45)

Comparing the Two Bodies

Paul compares the earthly and the heavenly body. The earthly body is perishable, sown in dishonor, in weakness and in a physical body. The heavenly body is imperishable, raised in glory, in power and in a spiritual body. A physical body proves there is a spiritual body, because the first Adam was a living being, but Christ is a life-giving spirit. The physical came first, followed by the spiritual (15:42-46).

Paul's teaching is more developed than Christ's. For Paul, man's heavenly life is connected with man's existence both "at the beginning" and in history. He turns his thoughts to "the beginning", to the present struggles of historical man, and to the reality of "the other world".

The Creation and Corruption Described in Genesis

Paul's teaching is rooted in the revealed mystery of the creation of man, an enlivening of matter by the spirit so that "the first man Adam became a living being" (Gen.15:45). Later, Genesis will show that sin caused the corruption of this body.

Paul uses words like "perishable", "weak", "in dishonor" (the consequences of sin). Elsewhere he speaks of "bondage to decay" (Rom.8:21). All of creation is subject to this "bondage to decay" because man's sins have both internal and cosmic effects. By these adjectives, Paul shows that the body expresses what creation is like after sin, and how it "has been groaning in travail together until now" (Rom.8:22).

Hope In Redemption – The Labor Pains of Birth

Just as labor pains accompany childbirth, so all creation "waits with eager longing for the revealing of the sons of God" and hopes to "be set free from its bondage to decay and obtain the glorious liberty of the children of God" (Rom.8:19-21).

Paul's interpretation of the resurrection sees the body of historical man as having both the "bondage of decay" and the hope which accompanies labor pains. This hope is rooted in the mystery of redemption which operates in man's soul by the first fruits of the Spirit. We groan inwardly waiting only for our adoption as sons,

109

the "redemption of our bodies" (Rom.8:23). Only the resurrection of the body fully accomplishes man's redemption.

January 27, 1982

71. THE HUMAN BODY – "OF EARTH" YET CAPABLE "OF HEAVEN"

Lessons From His Encounter With Christ
According to Paul (1Cor.15:42-49) the human body is seen as "incorruptible, glorious, full of dynamism and spiritual". By encountering Jesus in His glorified body, Paul learned the ultimate destiny of man and announces the "redemption of the body" (Rom.8:23) and the completion of that redemption (1Cor.15:42-49).

The Two Poles – The Two Dimensions
Paul's style uses many contrasts. He speaks of both the cosmic dimension and the personal dimension, of the "earthly man" and "the heavenly man". The mysteries of creation and redemption have placed every man between two poles which show the tension within man. "The first man was from earth, a man of dust: the second man is from heaven" (1Cor.15:47). Paul also explains God's actions within man, "As we have borne the image of the man of earth, so we will bear the image of the man of heaven" (5:49).

The Completion of Adam
The Risen Christ, the "man of heaven" is not the antithesis but the completion of Adam. He is the destiny willed for man by God from the beginning. The "man of earth" carries within himself a capacity for Christ. All men, while sharing in Adam's corruptible humanity, also have a capacity for incorruptibility.

Humanity appears ignoble and weak with an animal body. However, man's body contains an inner desire and a capacity for glory, the spiritual dynamism of the Risen Christ.

Capacity For Resurrection
For Paul, the word "body" means the total reality of human nature. Of all the bodies on earth, only the human body has this

110

capacity for resurrection and aspires to be incorruptible, glorious, and full of spiritual dynamism. Man alone is created in the image of God and in the image of the second Adam, Christ.

Paul's teaching is cosmic because every man bears the image of Adam and is also called to have the image of Christ. Although Paul writes about the future "We will bear the image of the man of heaven ..." (5:49) this reality already is a part of man and is meant to develop to its final completion.

Contrasting Paul and Christ

Although Paul's picture of the resurrected body is more detailed than Christ's, his sketch is more unilateral, focusing on the inner structure of the man-person. Christ's words (describing the person as totally divinized), show the Beatific Vision as the inexhaustible source of perpetual virginity and of the personal communion of those who share in the resurrection

February 3, 1982

72. PAUL'S VISION –
THE BODY'S POWER TO INHERIT HEAVENLY LIFE

Two Forces at Work

In his penetrating analysis of the forces within man, Paul contrasts the "earthly" (i.e. historical) man with the "risen man".

According to Paul, a radical transformation will take place. The body, which by nature is "perishable", "in dishonor" and "in weakness", will enter into a state of being "imperishable", "in glory" and "in power" (1Cor.15:42-45). "Weak", describes the body's beginning from the temporal soil and corresponds to the scientific word "semen" or seed.

Power to Inherit a "New Fullness"

Although like the animal body, the human body has an unusual capacity to inherit power from Christ. The human body can become a spiritual body, no longer subject to death. This transformation from weak to spiritual refers to the total constitution of the human person. The human body becomes spiritual. This is the source of the body's power over death.

For Paul, the future resurrection is more than a restoring of the body to its original state. Such a return to the previous innocent state does not follow the logic of redemption. Paul points to "a new fullness", which includes the drama of eating from the tree of knowledge.

The Power of the Spiritual Body

In man, as in an animal body, concupiscence prevails over the spiritual (1Cor.15:44). Although his animal body is condemned to death, man rises as a spiritual body when the Holy Spirit gains supremacy. The Spirit overcomes sensuality, those inner forces which limit the human spirit, tie it down, and restrict its power to know and love.

The "spiritual body" means the perfect sensitivity of the senses acting in full harmony with the human spirit. "Animal body" indicates sensuality as a prejudicial force which impels man toward evil.

Man's Choice

Man, the "living being" made up of body and soul, can choose to accept or to resist the Spirit of Christ. When he resists the Spirit, he does "the works of the flesh". When he accepts the Spirit, he brings forth the Spirit's fruits (Gal.5:22).

The Resurrection Mystery

St. Paul's teaching about man is permeated with the mystery of the resurrection, the definitive reception of the Holy Spirit. In Chapter 15, Paul describes the state of those who are fully unified by the Spirit with Christ's resurrection.

In reply to the Sadducees, Christ linked faith in the resurrection to the entire revelation of the God of Abraham, Isaac, Jacob and Moses. He then described the state of those who rose as "neither marrying nor given in marriage". Paul's description of the resurrection confirms Christ's teaching. *February 10, 1982*

Part Six
Christ's Teaching on
Virginity for the Sake of the Kingdom

73. CHRIST OFFERS A SURPRISING OPTION

Living the Resurrection While Still on Earth

Virginity or celibacy, the exclusive donation of self to God, is rooted in the Gospel soil of the theology of the body. When Christ said, "When they rise from the dead they neither marry nor are given in marriage" (Mt.12:35), He was speaking of a future life which has no marriage.

This heavenly life involves a full personal giving and a full personal intercommunion. These gifts come from the glorification of the body in eternal union with God. By a vocation to virginity, the person hears this call to heavenly life while still living on earth and able to "marry and be given in marriage" (Lk.20:34). Virginity, by a particular sensitivity, anticipates the future glory of resurrection.

The Basic Text (Mt.19:11-12)

Jesus spoke to the apostles, who had heard him telling the Pharisees that anyone who divorced his wife and married another committed adultery (Mt.19:8-9). They said, "If such is the case of a man with his wife, it is not expedient to marry" (19:10). Jesus responded, "Not all men can receive this precept, but only those to whom it is given. For there are eunuchs who have been so from birth, and there are eunuchs who have been made eunuchs by men, and there are eunuchs who have made themselves eunuchs for the sake of the kingdom of heaven. He who is able to receive this, let him receive it" (19:11-12).

Introducing a New Principle

Although the apostles asked about the expediency of not marrying when there was no possibility of divorce, Jesus spoke of a different theme. He introduced voluntary continence for the sake of the kingdom. This continence is not opposed to marriage nor does it judge marriage as unimportant.

Christ responded to the apostles' problem by referring to another principle. In choosing virginity, a person does not oppose marriage, but chooses a particular value. They discover and freely welcome the kingdom of heaven. Christ says clearly that "not all men can receive this" but "some are able" (19:11-12).

Orientation Toward Heaven

Christ's words are a counsel (received by some) and not a commandment (binding upon all). There is a particular grace ("to whom it has been given") and a personal choice ("those able to receive it"). The Holy Spirit gives this orientation toward the heavenly state, where men "neither marry nor are given in marriage".

However, a huge difference exists. In heaven, the absence of marriage will be everyone's fundamental state of existence. Here on earth, continence for the kingdom is an exception. On earth, "from the beginning" people "marry and are given in marriage".

Anticipating the Kingdom

However, Christ does not link his words on virginity to heaven (where people do not marry). His words to the Pharisees are about "in the beginning" and the indissolubility of the conjugal bond.

Virginity, therefore, is a call to an existence which is an exception to the state of historical man. This exception anticipates life in the Kingdom of Heaven. Virginity is not continence in the kingdom (the state of all men and women) but continence for the kingdom. Obviously, Jesus' words about virginity are linked to His description of the resurrection as "neither marrying nor giving in marriage".

By giving this supernatural purpose to the choice of virginity, Christ indicates the revelation in the Bible and in the rich spiritual tradition which has come forth in Church history.

March 17, 1982

114

74. VIRGINITY –
A CHALLENGE TO OLD TESTAMENT TRADITION

Three Classes of Eunuchs

Wanting to have His teaching accepted, Christ rooted this vocation to continence in the reality of earthly life, listing three categories of eunuchs. The first two categories concern physical defects, either congenital (19:11) or caused by human intervention (19:12). These two groups are involuntary states. The third group of "eunuchs" is voluntary ("have made themselves so") and supernatural ("for the sake of the kingdom") (19:12)..

Challenging the Old Testament Tradition

Formed by the Old Covenant, Christ's audience had no tradition of celibacy or virginity. (The only exception to the married state was physical impotence.) Therefore, Christ's words challenge the whole Old Testament. In the book of Judges, the daughter of Jephthah (who was destined to be sacrificed) said, "Let it be granted to me ... to bewail my virginity" (11:37). She does so for two months before returning to be sacrificed. The text ends, "She had never known a man" (11:39).

No Importance to Virginity

The Old Testament never gave any importance to virginity. No Old Covenant leader ever proclaimed continence, by word or example. Marriage had acquired a "consecrated significance" because God promised Abraham that he would be "the father of a multitude of nations", would be "extremely fruitful" and "kings shall come forth from you."(Gen.17:4,6-7). Because of procreation, the Old Testament made marriage a privileged state. The Messiah Himself would be the "son of David" (Mt.20:30). Marriage had everything in its favor and any ideal of continence was difficult to understand.

A Turning Point

Christ's words were a decisive turning point. His disciples had always associated virginity (especially in the male) with physical defects of nature. Jesus' reference to "eunuchs" evoked multiple associations of continence with physical defects only. In the kingdom, however, continence can be voluntarily chosen.

Matthew does not record the immediate reaction of the disciples. However, Paul (1Cor.7:25-40) confirms the impression made by Christ's words which have borne fruit in future generations (cf Rev.14:4). In speaking of continence "for" the kingdom, Christ stressed the supernatural motive in this choice and did not include any other motive. His words "for the kingdom" join this choice to a renunciation which requires spiritual effort.

March 17, 1982

75. MARY'S VIRGINITY – A SIGN OF THE SPIRIT'S FRUITFULNESS

A Heavenly Preview

Christ revealed that in heaven people "will no longer marry" (Mt.22:30). By this charismatic sign of virginity, some people choose to live here on earth as everyone will live in heaven. Virginity is a preview of the glorified man, who is totally united to God by a face-to-face vision and is united to everyone by the communion of saints.

Virginity shows that the body is meant for glorification, not for the grave. It shows the power of the redemption which Christ has placed in human history. Because Christ Himself freely chose this state, virginity bears His personal imprint.

Mary's Virginity – the Spirit's Fruitfulness

From the very beginning, Christ distanced Himself from the Old Testament view of the body. He was born of the Virgin Mary, who "did not know man" (Lk.1:34). Joseph did not hesitate to take Mary as his wife "for that which is conceived in her is of the Holy Spirit" (Mt.1:20).

First Witness to the Spirit

This virginal conception of Jesus was hidden from His contemporaries (who regarded Him as "the carpenter's son") and was far removed from the Old Testament tradition (which

116

exclusively favored marriage and rejected continence). Even though the Messiah was a son of David born according to the flesh, Mary and Joseph were the first witnesses of the fruitfulness of the Spirit. "That which is conceived in her is of the Holy Spirit" (1:20).

A Forerunner of Christ's Teachings
Although needed to be hidden from His contemporaries, Christ's birth is a preview of His later teaching. This mystery about the marriage of Joseph and Mary (revealed in the gospels of Matthew and Luke) concealed their perfect communion of persons and that continence for the kingdom which served the perfect fruitfulness of the Holy Spirit. Through the conditions of their pact, the Incarnation of the Eternal Word was realized, and the Son of God was conceived and born of the Virgin Mary.

Gradually Revealed
Mary's divine maternity is a superabundant revelation that in Jesus Christ, a human nature participates in the absolute fullness of the Spirit's fruitfulness. The virgin's divine maternity was gradually revealed to the Church. This indirectly aided the understanding of the sanctity of marriage and of the renunciation of marriage for the kingdom.

Christ's Example
When Christ first said these words, His own virginal conception and birth were unknown. However, Christ's example of His own virginity "for the kingdom" was an evident departure from the Old Testament tradition, (which gave exclusive value only to marriage). Only later, did the disciples see that continence reveals the fruitfulness of the Spirit. All of these gospel elements are found in Paul's writings.   *March 24, 1982*

76. CHOOSING THE PREFERRED WAY

Virginity Gains Preference
Christ wanted his disciples to see continence as one of the ways into His kingdom. Virginity, an absolute novelty in the Old

Testament, gained preference in the New Covenant. This has decisive significance for the theology of the body.

For the Kingdom

By His life and His words, Christ showed that virginity had a special value when it was "for the kingdom". He did not approach the question on a utilitarian level, as did the disciples who said, "If such is the case...it is not expedient to marry" (Mt.19:10). Christ showed that marriage retained a universal value, but that continence had a particular value and could be chosen "for the kingdom".

The Motivation – "For the Kingdom"

Christ highlights the motivation, the objective finality "of the kingdom". To rediscover continence as a fruitfulness of the Spirit, the person needs deep faith. He must identify himself with Christ's personal example, as a clear sign of "the other world". By virginity, human persons choose a special participation in the mystery of redemption, completing this mystery in their own flesh (Col.1:24).

In choosing continence, man must be motivated by this special participation in the redemption. Christ said that man is not obliged to virginity. He has a personal choice which is proper to a special call.

The Choice

"Not all men can understand it ..." (19:11), because understanding virginity is a grace. The choice is made after the person sees virginity's importance for the kingdom. Christ spoke of a man "making himself a eunuch". This is a firm choice of a fundamental state in his earthly life, a decision which must be renewed continually.

Christ did not hide the anguish of this decision and the enduring consequences for the person who retains the normal inclinations of his nature.

Virginity in the Context of Marriage

By this teaching, Christ opposed not only the whole Old Testament tradition but, in a certain sense, he opposed even the state of marriage ("in the beginning") to which He Himself had appealed. He, therefore, nuances His words. Man's state "in the beginning" shows the possibility of conceiving man as a solitary figure before God. However, God drew man out of this state saying, "It is not good for man to be alone ..." (2:18).

Christ, therefore, spoke of virginity in the context of marriage. By doing this, He taught that this double aspect of man (being male and female and meant for unity) remains man's essential reality. Yet, in this context, Christ deliberately spoke these words about virginity.

Marriage helps us to understand virginity for the kingdom, and virginity, by highlighting the mysteries of creation and of redemption, casts a light upon marriage. *March 31, 1982*

77. CALLED TO "BREAK AWAY FROM A CREATED GOOD"

Alone Before God

Christ fully accepted man as "dual" and yet "alone" before God. Continence, the call to solitude for God, respects the "dual nature of mankind", (the masculinity and femininity created for interpersonal communion), and preserves the integral truth of the person. Because Christ's teaching is radically new, the person must understand this important idea in order to accomplish the ideal of "making oneself a eunuch" and to be fully sincere in the choice.

Fulfilled in God's Communion of Persons

Continence does not lessen the value of marriage. The person has full awareness of the value of marriage and yet chooses to "break away from" those tendencies created by God which lead a man to marry. Continence is revealed to the man or woman as a specific call "for the kingdom". Christ's words call the person to virginity, even though his body still remains oriented for marriage.

In this call, the person discovers a solitude which is a fuller dimension of intersubjective communion. Achieving the kingdom requires an authentic development of God's image in Trinitarian communion. By choosing continence, a man knows he can fulfill himself in God's image and be a gift to others.

Two-fold Sacrifice

Continence, the voluntary giving up of matrimony, involves a renunciation of the conjugal union and a renunciation of procreation. Christ understood the importance of these sacrifices, both in light of the Jewish culture and of the value of matrimony itself. This "breaking away from a created good" demands daily self-sacrifices which are indispensable so that this fundamental choice lasts for a lifetime and becomes internally possible.

Continual Subjection to Christ's Redeeming Power

The same teaching about man underlies Christ's words about "looking with lust" and about voluntary continence. Every person carries within his body the heritage of sin and the heritage of redemption. Even after accepting voluntary continence, a person must continually subjugate his sinfulness to the power of redemption (just as a man who has chosen to marry must subjugate his sinfulness). However, the call to virginity places a greater responsibility because the person has chosen a greater good.

"Doing Well" and "Doing Better"

In describing continence as a vocation which is important for the kingdom, Christ implicitly stated that continence, in relation to the kingdom, is superior to marriage. Paul says those choosing matrimony do "well" and those choosing voluntary continence do "better" (1Cor.7:38).

However, the Church's tradition of the "superiority" of continence over matrimony does not belittle marriage's essential value, nor give support to Manichean teachings. The authentic Christian superiority comes from the motive, namely, "for the kingdom".   *April 7, 1982*

120

78. Two Faithful Paths Into the Kingdom

Superiority is Due to Motive
Christ's rich words place a proper limit on this subject, ruling out any inference that marriage is inferior with regard to the body. His teaching claims the superiority of continence because of the motive "for the kingdom", not because of abstinence from conjugal union. Continence is an ideal only for the sake of the kingdom.

Actually both marriage and continence are "for the kingdom" and are not opposed to one another, (as if they divide the Christian community into two camps, "the perfect" and "the less perfect"). All Christians, in both states, are oriented to the kingdom. However, continence has a particular importance and has much to teach to those who are married (and who constitute the majority of believers).

Perfection is Measured by Charity
The Church does not teach that unmarried persons, by reason of continence alone, are seen as "perfect", and married people as "imperfect". Although the Church has a state of perfection, this is based on three evangelical counsels (poverty, chastity and obedience) which correspond to Christ's call "to be perfect" (Mt.19:21).

Christian perfection is measured by charity. Even though the three evangelical counsels undoubtedly help people to reach charity, someone living in the world, (not even in a religious institute), can certainly reach a higher level of charity. By fidelity to these three counsels, everyone can reach perfection.

Two Faithful Directions
Therefore, in the perspective of the "heavenly Church", the choice of marriage or continence shows a complementarity, which corresponds to Christ's words about "eunuchs for the kingdom" (Mt.19:11-12). They complete and interpenetrate each other. Perfect conjugal love and lifelong virginity are both faithful directions into the kingdom. Both express a total gift and the conjugal meaning of the body.

Spiritual Paternity and Maternity
Virginity is analogous to conjugal love, because it must lead to paternity and maternity in the spiritual sense, which is a fruitfulness of the Spirit. On the other hand, physical procreation must have a spiritual paternity and maternity in the education of the children.

Obviously there are many aspects of complementarity. Paul teaches this when he writes, "Each has his special gift from God, one of one kind and one of another" (1Cor.7:7).

April 14, 1982

79. VERY FEW DETAILS ABOUT THE KINGDOM

The Objective Goal - Heaven
Christ's words, "for the sake of the kingdom of heaven", show the subjective motive of the call. However, the goal is objective, namely the kingdom in all its fullness

Christ preached that this kingdom is established in time and is completed in heaven. Christ taught (in His parable on the wedding banquet - Mt.22:1-14), that all are called to participate in the establishing of the kingdom. Those called to continence participate in a singular way in bringing about this kingdom on earth.

A Clear Display of the Redemption
Continence clearly displays the mystery of the redemption of the body because the self-renunciation (cf.Lk.9:23) reaches the point of renouncing marriage and a family. The person chooses virginity because he is convinced that continence is a greater contribution to establishing the kingdom on earth. Although Christ did not specify voluntary continence when speaking of "taking up the cross" (Lk.9:23), St. Paul did speak directly to this issue and the Church completed the teaching.

Unanswered Questions
Christ does not give a more detailed explanation of the relation between continence and the kingdom. He does not even say how these "eunuchs" are associated with the kingdom. All,

122

including "those who marry and are given in marriage", are in relation to the kingdom.

Christ's words also do not answer the question, "What is that kingdom for those who choose voluntary continence?" The disciples' question had a utilitarian attitude, "If this is the case ... it is better not to marry." (Mt.19:10). Christ evaded this aspect and refused to say "why" continence is better. He only said that continence has its own particular value and that those choosing continence must do so "for the kingdom" and not for a selfish calculation.

Marriage or Virginity – Chosen According to God's Plan

Christ's response also refers indirectly to his teaching on the indissolubility of marriage (Mt.19:3-9). To paraphrase, Christ said, "Whoever chooses marriage must choose it as God created it, "from the beginning", seeing the particular value in God's plan. Those who choose continence must do so because of the values proper to that vocation. Each must act in conformity with a chosen vocation."

The kingdom of heaven is the definitive fulfillment of all men's desires, and the fullness of God's bounty toward men. Many New Testament texts give further details about the kingdom. For those choosing continence, the important text is Ephesians 5:21-33, which is valid for both a theology of matrimony and a theology of virginity. (This is discussed fully in Part Seven.)

A Severity in His Words

Christ's words are characterized by a certain severity because He emphasizes the temporal realism of this decision to share in His redeeming work and show the gravity of this decision. Christ did not conceal that this choice is a renunciation which makes significant demands. By expressing this truth, His words have a convincing power.   *April 21, 1982*

80. VIRGINITY AFFIRMS THE NUPTIAL MEANING OF THE BODY

A Nuptial Response to Christ's Love

It is natural for the human heart to accept demands. In accepting virginity, the disciple sees that Christ, the Spouse of the Church and of souls, has given Himself completely to the human race. In response, the disciple accepts virginity. This is an act of nuptial love. Just as Christ's words about "in the beginning" led to a theology of the nuptial meaning of the body, so Christ's words on continence have a similar purpose.

Man's Clear Vision

In the modern mind, the sexual instinct is the same in animals and in the human person. However, Genesis (C.1 and 2) teaches a clear and univocal boundary between the world of animals and of man (who is created in God's image). Man has a clear awareness of what essentially distinguishes him from the animals.

Sexual Instinct – The Wrong Term

Therefore, this naturalistic category, "the sexual instinct" should not be applied to man, because he is "a rational animal". Even when applied analogously, we must set aside this naturalistic term, "sexual instinct", and use instead the true nuptial meaning of the body. This is discovered in the dual makeup of man and woman, masculine and feminine.

Knowing the Body's Nuptial Meaning

Only in this context, can Christ's words on continence for the kingdom be correctly understood. The basis of Christ's call is not the sexual instinct (somewhat the "naturalistic necessity") but the conscious freedom of man. In light of the body's nuptial meaning, Christ said, "He who is able to receive this, let him receive it." (Mt.19:12). Continence, although a gift, must be received. Each person has his own "I", especially in their reciprocal masculinity and femininity. This reciprocity is inscribed in human nature.

124

A Relationship "For" Another

Marriage is a reciprocal relationship "for" the other person. Christ's words show continence can also be "for" another. In marriage, a man rediscovers himself in the sincere gift of himself to another in "one flesh". A person who renounces this conjugal giving of himself to another person can give himself totally to Christ. In the nuptial meaning of the body, a man can commit himself to marriage or to the kingdom.

Knowing Before Choosing

Choosing marriage presupposes the knowledge and acceptance of the body's nuptial meaning. Choosing continence also requires a knowledge of the body's nuptial meaning. It comes about only as human persons fully realize their masculinity/ femininity. Christ clearly wanted the person to fully know and clearly choose when He said, "He who is able to receive this, let him receive it." (Mt.19:12).   *April 28, 1982*

81. AFFIRMING THE VALUE BY RENOUNCING IT – THE GOSPEL PARADOX

Needing A Realistic Knowledge

Christ said that God's original intention for marriage (Genesis, Chap. 1 and 2) conflicted with Moses' granting a decree of divorce. When His disciples said, "If this is the case of a man with his wife, it is not expedient to marry.", Jesus spoke of a conscious and voluntary renunciation of marriage. This is only possible if the person knows the value of the body's nuptial disposition to marriage. Choosing continence requires a realistic knowledge of what is renounced.

Affirming the Renounced Value

Virginity involves more than just "knowing" the value. Continence affirms the very value from which the unmarried person abstains. This is a gospel paradox, both eloquent and profound. Renouncing this value affirms the nuptial meaning of the human body and highlights this value. This is indispensable so that the nuptial meaning shines clearly in the ethos of conjugal life.

Those choosing continence exclude family life (which is chosen by most). However, this exclusion has great importance for the value and authenticity of family life itself. The sacramentality of marriage is understood through the special love of Christ for His Church (Eph.5:22-23). Christ, Himself a virgin, is the most perfect example.

An Unanswered Question

How is this call formed in the man on the basis of the knowledge of the body's nuptial meaning and the fruit of that knowledge? This question is important for the theology of the body and for the development of the human personality. However, an exhaustive answer would demand a study of the relationship between marriage and virginity which is beyond these present considerations.

A New Perspective

Continence is certainly a renunciation. However, it is also an affirmation which arises from a new personal realization of "being a gift for the other". Although identified with a renunciation of marriage, continence for the kingdom never denies marriage's essential value. Rather, it highlights the call to marriage and the dignity of the personal gift. Christ's call to continence is extremely important for Christian spirituality, for the study of man and for the theology of the body.   *May 5, 1982*

82. CHAPTER SEVEN OF FIRST CORINTHIANS

Answers Coming From Missionary Experience

In 1 Corinthians, Chapter 7, Paul presents Christ's teaching but gives it his own stamp. This personal interpretation is drawn primarily from the experiences of his missionary activity. He also had to answer concrete questions to ethical issues which surrounded Christian marriage and troubled the minds of his first Christian converts. These came more from pagan Hellenism than from Judaism.

126

In this letter, Paul uses both a magisterial and a pastoral tone and has a continuous conversation with his readers. Because he is a classical teacher of morality and resolves problems of conscience, moralists love to use his explanations and resolutions. However, Paul's bases his answers on Christ's teachings, not just on practical cases.

Paul's Opinion

Paul says that virginity is a counsel and not a commandment. "With regard to virgins, I have no command from the Lord, but I give an opinion." (7:25) His teaching is both a counsel and his personal opinion. He speaks to three groups: those already married, those who still must make that decision, and to widows.

The Two Cases

Paul describes someone who has strong passions and is not "behaving properly with regard to his betrothed". Paul writes, "Let him do as he wishes; he does not sin. Let them marry." (7:36). He also speaks of a person who "being under no necessity but having his desire under control" and "has determined in his heart, to keep her as his betrothed". Paul says "he will do well" to remain a virgin (7:37). His important sentence is, "So then, he who marries his betrothed does well, and he who refrains from marriage does better." (7:38).

Who Sought Advice?

The one seeking advice could have been a young man facing a decision to marry, or a newlywed seeking direction in his marriage (in face of the asceticism in the Church of Corinth) or a parent (guardian) of a girl, (because in those days parents made the decisions). Paul certainly answers that the decision about continence must be voluntary and only voluntary continence is better than marriage.

Good and Better

Therefore, voluntary continence is a counsel and, given the appropriate circumstances, is better than marriage. There is no question of sin. Paul says that this is not a question between good and evil but between good and better. (This question might have come from dualistic teaching that later became Manichaeism.) From these words, we can make no judgment about Paul's thinking on marriage. This will be partially explained in Corinthians (Ch.7) and more fully explained in Ephesians (5:21-33).

June 23, 1982

83. ANXIOUS TO PLEASE THE LORD

The Time is Short

Paul explains why a decision for continence is better than a choice of marriage. He says that the time is short, that "the form of this world is passing away", and his believers are "to be free from anxieties" (7:29-32).

Difficulties in Marriage

Paul speaks of his own experience of celibacy, "I wish that all were as I myself am." (7:17). To the married, he writes "Yet they will have troubles in the flesh, and I would want to spare you that." (7:28). He had already expressed this opinion when he wrote "Now concerning the matters about which you write, it is well for a man not to touch a woman." (7:1).

No Easy Task

Christ spoke of a woman in childbirth having "afflictions" but who would rejoice in her newborn child (Jn.16:21). Here, Paul writes of "the tribulations of the body" which spouses will experience. Paul has no personal aversion to marriage but warns young people who might believe that conjugal union will bring only happiness.

Frequently, spouses are disappointed in their expectations. The joy of their union is accompanied by "troubles in the flesh". These are often moral troubles and Paul teaches that he who "cleaves to his wife and the two become one flesh" does not have an easy task.

Christ and Paul

In speaking of continence, Christ never pointed out the troubles of marriage. Instead, He highlights the painful choice of continence by which a man makes himself a "eunuch".

Paul expresses this gift differently. He writes, "I tell you this, brothers, the time is already short" and "the form of this world is passing away" (7:29 and 31). The perishability of human existence and of the temporal world leads to the conclusion that "those who have wives should live as though they had none" (7:29).

A Different Approach

While Christ emphasized the greatness of the renunciation, Paul stresses what the kingdom should mean to the person. Christ speaks of a man becoming a "eunuch" for the sake of the kingdom. Paul uses the word "unmarried" and describes the person's goals. "The unmarried person is anxious about the affairs of the Lord, how to please the Lord." (7:32)

Anxiety For the Churches

Luke, Paul's disciple, said that believers must be anxious only in seeking the kingdom of God (12:31). They must seek "the one thing necessary" (10:41). Paul is anxious "for all the churches" (2Cor. 11:28) and cares for the members of Christ's Body (Phil.2:20-21 and 1Cor.12:25). There are many "anxieties" in the kingdom to which the unmarried man can give his heart.

The "Affairs of the Lord"

Paul highlights anxiety "about the affairs of the Lord". This is a concise expression of the kingdom. These "affairs of the Lord" extend to everything because "The earth is the Lord's and everything in it." (10:26).

"Lord" describes Jesus Christ (Phil.2:11). The "affairs of the Lord" are the Church and its growth. Because the unmarried person is anxious about the Church, Paul says, "I wish that all of you were as I myself am." (7:7).

Care for the World

Apostolic zeal does not exhaust Paul's motivation for continence. "To please the Lord" embraces every aspect of man's personal relationship to God. Jesus Himself said, "I always do what is pleasing to him (the Father)" (Jn.8:29), and Paul confirms that Christ "did not please himself" (Rom.15:3).

These two aspects overlap. "To please the Lord" must involve a care for all that "pertains to the Lord". The believer is not "closed in" but is "open to the world". *June 30, 1982*

84. AN INVITATION TO CONFRONT PAGAN CORINTH

Divided and Undivided

Paul writes about "The unmarried person, who is anxious ... how to please the Lord" (1Cor.7:32) and about the married person, "who is anxious ... how he may please his wife" (7:33). Man is naturally inclined to please the one he loves. Therefore, "to please God" has the spousal character of an interpersonal relationship. God approves this aspiration of man "to please" Him. Even the desire itself is a gift from God.

Undivided

The man bound by marriage "is divided" by family obligations (7:34). Apparently, the unmarried man has an inner unification, allowing him complete dedication to the kingdom. His motives must be "for the kingdom". "Division" and "emptiness" can enter into the unmarried person if he is deprived both of marriage and of any clear reason for renouncing marriage.

Not Without Difficulties

Paul, realizing this, doesn't force anyone into virginity. He gives advice so the unmarried are united to the Lord without distractions (7:35). Jesus was aware that the apostles "continued with me in my trials" (Lk.22:28). Jesus is a "high priest" who can "sympathize with our weakness" (Heb.4:15). The problems of the unmarried are part of the great stream of Christ's sufferings. Paul's goal is "adherence to the Lord without distraction." (7:35).

To Be Holy – Separated From the Profane

Paul gave the same teaching when he said that the unmarried woman "is anxious about the affairs of the Lord, in order to be holy in body and spirit" (7:35).

In the Bible, "to be holy" is a state rather than an action. The person is separated from whatever is profane so as to belong exclusively to God. Holiness "in body and spirit" presupposes behavior "without spot or wrinkle", as the Church is in Christ's presence (Eph.5:27).

Conflict With Pagan Corinth

Paul is deeply human as he proclaims an order of values which conflict with the pagan world of Corinth.

He appeals to those Corinthians who were "using the world" (Marriage is "using the world".) to live "as though they had no dealings with it" (7:31). In Corinth, marriage was understood differently from the whole Jewish tradition. By encouraging abstinence, Paul highlights an understanding of the gospel's order of values.

Free to Choose

He says to the unmarried and to the widows "It is good for them to remain as I am". However, he adds, "But if they cannot live in continence, let them marry" (7:8-9). He had counseled earlier that "It is well for a man not to touch a woman" but because of the danger of incontinence, "each man should have his own wife and each woman her own husband" (7:1-2).

Not Just A Remedy For Concupiscence

These words make it appear that Paul sees marriage only as a remedy for concupiscence (a traditional theological phrase). However, Paul wrote later "but each has his own special gift from God, one of one kind and one of another" (7:7). Those who choose marriage, therefore, have their proper gift which is suited for their vocation.

Although Paul emphasizes marriage as a "remedy for concupiscence", he also sees its charismatic character. There is an action of grace in both the married and the unmarried.

July 7, 1982

85. MARRIAGE, THE WORLD AND HEAVEN

The World is "Passing Away"
Paul declares that the person who chooses virginity does better than the one who chooses marriage because "the world is passing away". This teaching, focusing on the transient nature of the world, has greater power than the argument based on heaven.

Paul says that this world is not man's eternal destiny, and marriage is tied to "the form of this world which is passing away". Paul, like Christ, foresees a resurrection in which people do not marry. Therefore, Christians must realize that marriage is part of a transient world. Abstention from marriage frees the person from this "passing nature". However, this motivation is secondary. Paul's main reason for virginity is that the unmarried are "anxious about the affairs of the Lord".

Honoring the Body as a Temple of the Spirit
Concerning widows, Paul says they are free to marry but he would be happier "if she remains as she is" (7:39-40). Although teaching that "Your body is a temple of the Holy Spirit who is in you" (6:19), Paul is fully aware of the body's weaknesses due to the "concupiscence of the flesh".

God's gift is shared by both the unmarried and the married. One is not "spiritual" and the other "carnal", because both receive a gift from God. Their bodies are temples of the Holy Spirit and those who remain faithful to their gift do not dishonor the Spirit's temple.

The Rights of the Married
Married life is a gift and conjugal relations are subject to this gift of marriage. "The husband should give to his wife her conjugal rights and likewise the wife to her husband". Paul's reasons are clear. "The wife does not rule over her own body, but

the husband does; likewise, the husband does not rule over his own body, but the wife does" (7:3-4).

Paul's words "rights" and "does not rule" can be explained only in the context of the sacramental covenant of marriage (cf. Eph.5:22-33).

In First Corinthians, Paul advises married couples not to refuse conjugal rights "except perhaps by mutual consent for a time". He advises them "to come together again lest Satan tempt you through lack of self control. I say this by way of concession, not of command" (7:5-6). These are significant texts. By referring to a "concession", he teaches that both conjugal relations and periodic abstinence are God's gifts by which couples strengthen their mutual bond.

An Idealism Which is Pastoral

Paul's rule of "concession" shows the different subjective responses of the man and the woman, which are both spiritual and emotional. The person's sensitivity to the other must always remain under the gift received from God.

Paul has pastoral wisdom and gospel idealism. He bases his teaching on virginity and marriage on the truth that man, with his body, is destined for eternal life. He encourages both virginity and marriage, (two dimensions of the human vocation) because both show the nuptial meaning of the body, masculine and feminine.

Therefore, the theology of the body is needed for a study of man so that a correct set of norms can become clear.

July 14, 1982

86. AWAITING THE BODY'S REDEMPTION

Redemption – An Immediate Gift After Sin

Paul teaches the redemption of the body in both a personal and a cosmic dimension. His words, "We groan inwardly as we await … the redemption of our body" (8:23) show the personal dimension. His teaching "Creation awaits with eager longing the revelation of the sins of God" (Rom.8:19) shows the cosmic dimension.

Personal and Cosmic

The redemption of the body is a hope which was immediately placed within man after the first sin. God promised an enmity between Satan and the woman and between Satan's "offspring and her offspring" (Gen.3:15). This is the first announcement of salvation. Therefore, the redemption of the body was given from the beginning and is part of all creation, which has always been subordinated to man (Gen.1:28-30).

Man At the Center

In presenting redemption's cosmic dimension, Paul places man at the center, just as God placed man at creation's center. Man has the "first fruits of the Spirit" and "groans inwardly" awaiting his redemption" (8:23). Christ, by His death and resurrection, is the historical source of redemption and we await in hope its definitive heavenly fulfillment.

Christ's Teaching Explains Paul's Doctrines

The theology of the body, based on Christ's teaching about "the beginning", about the indissolubility of marriage, about concupiscence of the flesh and about the future resurrection of the body, is needed to understand Paul's "redemption of the body". Christ speaks to man who is subject to concupiscence and yet is destined for resurrection.

Meaning of "Body"

In Genesis and in Paul, "body" is the visible aspect of man, who belongs to the visible world. For Paul, "body" has an additional meaning. It is an alienation of man from visible creation because of the Spirit's influence. Both meanings are in relation to the body's resurrection.

Paul says we await the "redemption of our bodies" the victory over death won by Christ's resurrection. Abstaining from marriage is done for the kingdom established by Christ's resurrection.

The Daily Victory

The redemption of the body is not just victory over death. It also overcomes the evil of concupiscence and allows man to live in indissoluble marriage. Redemption is a daily victory over sin and is the hope of every day.

From the mystery of redemption, man draws power to overcome concupiscence, and woman receives help in living an indissoluble marriage. This daily hope overcomes "evil with good" (Rom.12:21). By manifesting itself in the human heart, redemption clears man's path for the heavenly glory.

This redemption results in a daily morality and helps to overcome concupiscence. It reveals the person's dignity and highlights the body's nuptial meaning. Because of redemption, man can enjoy a mature freedom and express it both in marriage and in virginity.   *July 21, 1982*

Part Seven
The Crowning Text – Ephesians 5:21-33

87. EPHESIANS - GOD'S PLAN REVEALED

Paul's text in Ephesians (5:21-33) is the crowning words of the theology of the body and must be interpreted in light of what was said by Christ when He revealed the beginning gift of original innocence, the concupiscence in the man of lust, and, finally, the body's future resurrection. All of this theology is viewed as "the redemption of our body" (Rom 8:23).

Two Meanings of "Body"
Paul's words in Ephesians center on the body in two ways. He uses "body" in the metaphorical meaning of the Church (as the Body of Christ) and in the concrete meaning of the human body (masculine and feminine) destined for union in marriage.

Why and in what way do these two meanings of "body" appear in the text? An analysis will yield central themes and essential truths based upon the full biblical context.

Gradual Answers
Because the liturgy associates this Ephesians text with the sacrament of marriage, we will see how this truth about the sacrament emerges and is confirmed. These answers will come gradually.

Besides referring to "the beginning", Paul also describes the relations between Christ and His Church in themes of the Old Testament prophets who saw God having "spousal love" for His people. We need to examine these texts in light of all that we have learned about the theology of the body

The Body and Sacrament
Because the sacrament and the body are both "visible signs" of an invisible reality, the body enters into the definition of "sacrament", that is, an efficacious sign indicating and producing

136

grace. God gives himself to man through sacraments, fulfilling in him the work of salvation.

Although we already have a direction, we also need to go beyond the text to understand all that God has revealed in these words. This text "reveals man to man and makes him aware of his lofty vocation" (Gs. 22) because he shares in the mystery of Christ.

July 28, 1981

88. AN OVERVIEW OF THE EPHESIANS LETTER

Definite Structure of Ephesians

We need to examine how Ephesians 5:21-33 is situated in the entire letter. Although scholars debate many questions, Ephesians clearly has a very significant structure. The author presents God's plan for the salvation of man in Jesus Christ. He says that God has chosen man to be "holy and blameless before him" and has destined man "to be his sons through Jesus Christ".

This was "freely bestowed on us in the Beloved", through whom we have "redemption through his blood, the forgiveness of our trespasses". All of this is God's "plan for the fullness of time to unite all things in him" (1:3,4-7, 10).

Christ As Head

Having presented God's plan and its fulfillment, Ephesians asks us to see Christ as the head of the Church. "He has made him the head over all things for the Church, which is his body, the fullness of him who fills all in all" (1:22-23).

In Christ, Gentiles and Jews are called to join together as in a temple (2:11-21). Paul especially prays for Gentiles, "bending his knee before the Father" and asking that they "be strengthened with might through his Spirit in the inner man" (3:14-16).

Instructions on Christian Life

Then, Paul gives more detailed instructions aimed at defining the Christian life as a vocation flowing from this divine plan. He touches on many valid questions, exhorting his readers to the preservation of unity, which is constructed by the multiple diversity of Christ's gifts. He summons believers to overcome vices and to acquire virtues according to their vocation in Christ (4:21-32). "Therefore, be imitators of God, as beloved children" (5:1).

More Detailed Instructions

In the fifth chapter, his directives become more detailed. The author condemns pagan abuses, telling his readers that they once were in darkness but are now "light in the Lord" and should "walk as children of the light" (5:8). He tells them "not to be foolish" and not "to get drunk with wine". Instead they are "to be filled with the Spirit, addressing one another in psalms and hymns and spiritual signs ..." (5:17-19). He describes the climate of the spiritual life needed in the Christian community, and then speaks to the domestic community, the family. "Be filled with the Spirit. Be subject to one another out of reverence for Christ" (5:20-21).

Now we arrive at our text, (Ephesians 5: 21-33), which is placed within two central teachings. First, Paul says that the mystery of Christ is realized in the Church. Secondly he writes that the Christian vocation must correspond to this mystery of Christ.

All Family Members

This Christian vocation is lived by all the family members, not just by husband and wife. "Children, obey your parents in the Lord, for this is right. Honor your father and mother ... Fathers, do not provoke your children to anger but bring them up in the discipline and instruction of the Lord" (6:1-4). There are duties "of servants to masters and masters to servants" (6:5-9). The family, then, includes servants or slaves of both sexes.

Although the immediate context is the moral obligation of the family (the "domestic codes") the crowning text itself (5:21-33) deals exclusively with married couples and marriage.

The whole letter ends with an encouragement to spiritual warfare (6:10-20), (which is an explicit fulfillment of the guidelines), with brief recommendations (6:21-22) and farewell (6:23-24). *August 4, 1982*

138

89. THE GREAT ANALOGY OF MUTUAL SUBJECTION

A Double Reverence
Be "subject to one another out of reverence for Christ" (5:21), speaks of a double relationship. The couple has a relationship with Christ and with each other. "Reverence for Christ" is analogous to "fear of God". This reverence (The Old Testament word was "piety".) is not a defensive attitude in the face of evil but a respect for "the body".

The spouses' own relationship must be based on a profound awareness of the mystery of Christ because their entire conduct is deduced from this mystery. As this mystery penetrates them and leads them to a "reverence for Christ", they can "be subject to one another" because they have been chosen by Christ for partnership in marriage.

Mutual Subjection Is Not Unilateral Domination
After speaking of their "mutual subjection", Paul writes "Wives, be subject to your husband, as to the Lord" (5:22). The husband is not "lord" of the wife and certainly he has no right of "domination". The wife should find the motivation of her relationship to her husband in her relationship to Christ. This flows from the very essence of marriage. The relationship is not a "one-sided domination" because the spouses are to be "subject to one another", the fruit of piety.

To alleviate fears, Paul immediately writes, "Husbands, love your wives." True love excludes any possibility of unilateral domination, and the husband is also to be subject to his wife. Marriage is a reciprocal donation and a mutual subjection, of which Christ is the model. This describes a spiritual maturity, bringing about a new fusion of bilateral conduct.

Ephesians and Modern Culture
Paul accepts the concepts of his first century Ephesian readers who knew the subjection of wife to husband. However, he believes that, "out of reverence for Christ", the couple will establish a just balance.

Although our modern culture is quite different, the Ephesian principle should produce the same result. "Mutual subjection out of reverence for Christ" provides a solid structure for family unity.

Paul lists much more than the traditional moral teachings. He discovers the mystery of Christ in the marital relationship, for "Christ, is the head of the Church" and has "loved the Church". Although the man is head of the wife, he must love his wife "as Christ loved the Church" (5:22-25). For Paul, the moral teaching is seen as part of God's eternal plan in Christ.

The Great Analogy

Ephesians presents this as "the great analogy". The first part is the wives' subjection to their husband "as to the Lord" (because the husband is head of the family as Christ is head of the Church). The second part is that the wives be subject "as the Church is subject to Christ". There are two models - Christ's relationship to the Church and the Church's relationship to Christ. This same analogy permeates the entire text (Eph.5:21-33). All mutual relationships are enlightened by Christ's relationship with His Church. *August 11, 1982*

90. THE ANALOGY REVEALS RELATIONSHIPS

Marriage Unveils God's Mystery

The reciprocal relationship of the spouses is an image of the relationship of Christ with His Church. Using this marital relationship, Paul reveals the mystery of God's love which has been hidden for all eternity. This is most clearly expressed by an analogy of the conjugal love between Christ and His Church. This analogy complements the mystery of the Mystical Body (Eph.1:22-23) in which Paul attempts to express God's eternal love for man.

Christ's Conjugal Love

Christ's Mystical Body illuminates the mystery of His conjugal love for the Church. This analogy unveils the essential truth that marriage corresponds to the vocation of Christians only when it reflects the love of Christ the Bridegroom and the attempt

140

of His wife, (the Church), to return to Christ. This is God's "redeeming love" for man. "Even as he chose us in him before the foundation of the world, that we should be holy and blameless before him" (1:4).

The Analogy Exhorts and Reveals

These texts have an exhortative tone. "As the Church is subject to Christ, so let wives be subject in everything to their husbands" and "Husbands love your wives, as Christ loved the Church ..." (5:24-25). The texts show that marriage shares in the mystery of Christ and the Church.

The analogy reveals the essence of Christ's relationship with the Church and the essence of marriage. The analogy also shows how marriage emerges from the mystery of God's eternal love, and provides a deeper understanding of the Church and of marriage itself.

Our Analysis

First, we will analyze marriage in light of Christ's spousal relationship to the Church. This will show how marriage is a visible sign of God's eternal love and will lead us to the foundations of the sacramentality of marriage

The Church is Saved by Submission

Paul explains that the wife's submission to her husband, "out of reverence for Christ", is part of a reciprocal submission. He then says that "the husband is the head of the wife as Christ is the head of the Church, his body, and is himself its Savior" (5:23). He is head as "Savior of his Body".

In being submissive to Christ, the Church becomes His Body and receives the fullness of salvation because Christ "gave himself up for her" (5:25). By His obedience unto death, Christ formed the Church as His Body. As head, He is the Church's Savior, and, as Savior, He is the Church's Head. As Savior and Head, Christ is the Bridegroom of the Bride.

The Redeemer Becomes the Bridegroom

Christ's Body, the Church, receives the entire gift of salvation, the fruit of Christ's own self-giving. Christ's redeeming love is transformed into spousal love. By His redeeming act, Christ is united once and for all as Bridegroom with His bride.

The redemption of the body conceals within itself the mystery of the "marriage of the Lamb" (Rev.19:7). Through Christ as Head, the full Redemption gift penetrates the Church and forms Her life. In this spousal form of the analogy, the head/body relationship becomes the groom/bride relationship.

August 18, 1982

91. EXAMINING ANOTHER ANALOGY – HEAD AND BODY

The analogy of head and body confers a meaning upon the Church, which is formed by Christ into His own Body. The union of body with head is organic. The psychic oneness, the unity of the human person, is based upon this organic union because the body lives by the head and vice-versa.

An Analogy Within An Analogy

Although speaking about Christ and the Church, the author has introduced this head/body analogy within his analogy of marriage. The author speaks of the husband as "head of the wife" and the wife as "the body of the husband", as if they form a biological union, (the "one flesh" mentioned in Genesis 2:24). In Genesis, the man and woman are two distinct persons who knowingly decide on their conjugal union. This is also true in Ephesians.

Becoming One

This analogy of "head-body" deals with two distinct subjects. However, by their reciprocal relationship, they become a single subject, as the head with the body constitutes a human person. Christ, although a subject different from His Church, has a reciprocal relationship with His Church, as in the union of head and body. The Church discovers herself only through her mystical union with Christ. This is true also of the spouses as "the two become one flesh" (5:31).

Not Blurred but Contained

The individuality of the persons (the basis for the "one single body" image) is not blurred but is contained in the image of Christ as Head of the Church. The Church, the Body of Christ, is clearly a second subject, to whom Christ shows His love. In like manner, the husband must love his wife so the two are subject to each other "out of reverence for Christ".

Becoming One Through Spousal Love

Although "Be subordinate to one another"(5:21) shows their bisubjectivity, the full text shows also a "single body" image. This image of the "single body" is a model of a husband's love for his wife. "Christ loved the Church and gave himself up for her that he might sanctify her." (5:25-26) He purified the Church by Baptism, "the washing of water with the word" (5:26). This washing is filled with Christ's redemptive power and brings about the purification of the Church by which she acquires a spousal character.

The Baptismal Bath – A Wedding Preparation

The author sees that Christ's spousal love is applied to His Church at every person's Baptism. By Baptism, every person shares in Christ's spousal love. The "washing of water with the word" prepares the Bride for the Bridegroom.

Baptism makes the Church a spouse, both "in the first act" and in the distant perspective of heaven. Christ does this washing "to present the Church to himself in splendor" (5:27). "To present" is the wedding moment. As the bride is led in, the groom is concerned that she should be beautiful. However, Baptism is only the beginning. The truly glorious Church will only emerge as the fruit of redemptive and spousal love at Christ's final coming.

August 25, 1982

143

92. A BRIDE WHO IS ETERNALLY YOUNG AND BEAUTIFUL

Christ Redeems His Body

The relationship of husband and wife is an analogy of the spousal bond between Christ and His Church. The Church is seen as a bride, all-beautiful in her body. The metaphor shows the importance of the body, which is "without spot or wrinkle" (5:27). "Spot" is a sign of ugliness and "wrinkle" is a sign of old age or senility. Both terms indicate moral defects, sin. Paul uses "old man" as a term for sinful man (Rom.6:6). Christ's redemptive love guarantees that the Church will be sinless and "eternally young".

The Beautiful Body

By references to the human body, this vast metaphor indicates the moral, spiritual and supernatural qualities of the Church. The Church has the body of a bride who is free from ugliness and old age, "holy and without blemish". This Church welcomes her Bridegroom who "has loved the Church and has given himself for her", a spiritual reality described by bodily features.

Christ's love is a model for every bridegroom's love for his wife. Love obliges the husband to be solicitous for his wife, to appreciate her beauty and to care for her. The bridegroom has a loving anxiety to discover his bride's beauty and by his love creates good within her.

Becoming One Flesh

The "one flesh" theme of Genesis reappears. "Husbands should love their wives as their own body" (5:28). They are not one person because their unity is only intentional. The wife's body is not the husband's body but must be loved like his own.

This unity through love is even more confirmed. "He who loves his wife loves himself" (5:28). By love, the "I" of the wife becomes also the "I" of the husband. The body is the expression of that "I" and their union is expressed through the body.

Later, the author, instead of the word "husband", uses the phrase "He who loves his wife" (5:28). The wife is called "she who is loved". The wife's experiences her husband's love by her submission, just as the Church experiences Christ's love by Her submission. The Bride, the object of Christ's redemptive love, becomes His Body. By Christ's spousal love, the Church becomes "one flesh" with Him.

First A Spouse

This moral unity brings about a spiritual belonging so that, "He who loves his wife loves himself" (5:28). The opposite possibility is excluded, "For no man hates his own flesh" (5:29), but "He nourishes and cherishes it (his own body) as Christ does the Church, because we are members of his body" (5:36). Through love, the other person's body becomes one's own. While describing "carnal" conjugal love, the words really speak the language of "agape".

Also a Parent

"Nourishes and cherishes" (5:29) show a protective relationship, a parental love. Christ protects His Church and "nourishes" her in the Eucharist. These "minor key" expressions, show the specific character of spousal love, the dignity of the body and the moral imperative to seek its good. Seeing the Church as the Body of Christ shows the "sacredness" of the human body and of marriage, (in which the reciprocal relationship of the body takes place). *September 1, 1982*

93. THE MYSTERY IS REVEALED IN PHASES

Linked to Genesis and Creation

Ephesians (5:31) quotes from Genesis (2:24). "For this reason a man shall leave his father and mother and be joined to his wife and the two shall become one flesh". This text provides the foundation of the mystery of Christ's relationship with His Church. Marriage, the most ancient way that God revealed His plan of salvation, is united with Christ, the definitive revelation of that plan. "Christ loved the Church and gave himself up for her" (5:25).

Revealing the Mystery

God's salvific plan, hidden from eternity, is highlighted by the words "This is a great mystery, and I mean in reference to Christ and the Church" (5:32). Here "mystery" signifies the plan of God which has been hidden and later revealed in history. This is the "great mystery", the central theme of all revelation which God wants to transmit to man.

Phases of the Mystery

God initiated this saving work which culminates in man's union with God. Paul highlights the continuity of the Old Covenant (established when God constituted marriage in creation), with the New Covenant, (established when Christ gave Himself for his Bride). This continuity shows that the "great mystery" passed through different phases of manifestation, beginning with creation and accomplished in "the fullness of time" (Gal.4:4).

Sacrament and Mystery

Does the author see this "great mystery" as a sacrament, especially the sacrament of marriage? Although not saying this directly (as scripture scholars agree) he does give the basis for the sacramentality of the Christian life, and specifically of marriage.

Proclaiming and Accomplishing

Is not "sacrament" synonymous with "mystery"? A sacrament presupposes the revelation of the "mystery" and its acceptance by faith. The sacrament "manifests" the mystery in a sign. It proclaims the mystery and accomplishes the mystery within the believer. Through the sacrament (a visible, efficacious sign of grace) the mystery of God's call is accomplished in man. Although still "veiled", the sign "makes visible" the supernatural mystery working within man.

Was Hidden – Now Accomplished

The mystery "hidden in God" is now the mystery "accomplished by Christ". Christ has redeemed the Church and is united with her in a "spousal manner". Vatican Council II said, "The Church is in Christ in the nature of a sacrament – a sign and instrument, that is, of communion with God and of unity among all men" (LG. 61). The text says that the Church is "in the nature of a sacrament". Speaking of the Church as "sacrament" is analogical and is not identical with the seven sacraments administered by the Church.

The Church's sacramentality is constituted by all the sacraments through which she sanctifies. The Church is the source of the sacraments, especially Baptism and Eucharist, and has a particular relationship with marriage, the most ancient sacrament.

September 8, 1982

94. CALLED INTO THE MYSTERY OF CHRIST

Once Hidden

This mystery has been hidden for ages in God "who has blessed us in Christ with every spiritual blessing in the heavenly places". "He destined us in love to be his sons through Jesus Christ". This is a "glorious grace which He freely bestowed on us in the Beloved" (1:3-6).

Now Fulfilled

Having spoken of the mystery hidden for ages (3:9) Ephesians describes the fulfillment phase, as Christ's gift becomes a part of man. "In him we have redemption through his blood, the forgiveness of our trespasses ..." (1:7). "He has made known to us this mystery" (1:9). This is "a plan for the fullness of time to unite all things in him" (1:10).

The time for revelation came in Christ, so that in Him "all things might be united, things in heaven and things on earth". This is the goal of all history and the author exhorts all believers, especially husbands and wives, to model their lives on Christ.

The Mystery and the Sacramental Order

The author always refers to this mystery, and links moral aspects to the sacramental order. "In him you also, who have heard the word of truth, the gospel of your salvation, and have believed in him, were sealed with the promised Holy Spirit." (1:13).

The sacramental order is certainly present, because the author writes to the baptized members of the ecclesial community. Ephesians 5:21-33 is important in understanding the relationship of this mystery with the sacramentality of marriage.

Christ is the Gift

Christ is at the heart of this mystery because, in Christ, humanity has received "every spiritual blessing". We were chosen in Christ "before the creation of the world". Through Christ, "We have redemption through his blood" (1:7). By accepting Christ, we participate in God's eternal mystery. This supernatural conferring of redemption results from Christ's spousal devotion to His Church (5:21-33). Christ Himself is the gift.

Linked to Old Testament Prophets

This classic text on Christ's spousal love for His Church is in continuity with the Old Testament, especially those prophetic texts which described Yahweh's spousal love for Israel. Unfortunately, Yahweh's love was not returned. Israel fell into infidelity and a worship of strange gods.

The prophets called this "the adultery of Israel". The analogy of the spouses (used to define Christ's relationship to the Church) finds an abundant tradition in the Old Testament. A special example of this is Isaiah (54:4-10) which is treated in the next chapter. *September 15, 1982*

95. ISAIAH'S ANALOGY IS FULLY REVEALED IN EPHESIANS

Because Isaiah 54:4-10 contains no reproaches to Israel as an unfaithful spouse, the biblical analogy (husband/wife) becomes more evident. Yahweh's love is a spouse's love for his wife. "Your maker is your husband." (54:5). This is how Isaiah explains the events in Israel's history. This is the same direction given by Ephesians which was based upon the already accomplished redemption.

148

God Removes Any Reproach

Isaiah has the colorful tradition and mentality of the Old Testament. God addresses Israel just as a husband speaks to his wife. He underlines His choice to take away the woman's "dishonor", brought about by virginity or widowhood. "You will forget the shame of your youth and the reproach of your widowhood you will remember no more." (54:4) He also removes the reproach of the adulterous wife who has been sent away. "The Lord has called you like a wife forsaken and grieved in spirit, like a wife of youth when she is cast off." (54:6).

Initiation By God

The text speaks of the "love of compassion". This phrase shows the social nature of Old Testament marriage and that God's love comes totally from His own initiative. Grace is contained in that love from the very beginning and is linked to faithfulness forever.

Isaiah calls the Creator/God the "spouse" of His Chosen People. "for your Maker is your husband" (54:5) and speaks of a lasting compassion "... my steadfast love shall not depart from you" (54:8). The text has an extraordinary richness when it says "The Holy One of Israel is your Redeemer" (54:5).

A Greater Richness

Although both Isaiah and Ephesians use the analogy of spousal love, they have diverse theological viewpoints. Ephesians sees the mystery of election taking place as "God the Father of our Lord Jesus Christ" embraces mankind in His Son. Mankind has a call "to be holy and blameless before him" (1:1). This is the mystery of adoption, "He destined us to be his adopted sons through Jesus Christ." (1:5). This richness in Paul shows that Isaiah's analogy constitutes only a part of the theological prospective. Ephesians has an added image, the paternity of God.

Ephesians Deepens Isaiah's Teachings

Spousal love appears only as the Creator is seen as Redeemer "For your Maker is your husband ... the Holy One of Israel is your Redeemer" (54:5).

Ephesians develops fully this idea of the "Redeemer", the "beloved Son" in whom we have redemption (Eph.1:6-7). This Son has given Himself up for His Church (5:25). Isaiah's "Creator Lord of hosts" becomes Paul's "Holy One of Israel", the Redeemer of the New Israel. Truly, Ephesians deepens and transforms Isaiah by the revealed doctrines of the Trinity and of Christ's role in Redemption.

Fully Revealed

Ephesians doesn't repeat "Your Maker is your husband" but shows the Redeemer giving himself up in spousal love. Paul transforms Isaiah's analogy. Isaiah scarcely outlines this mystery. With him, it is only "half-opened". Ephesians totally reveals the fullness of the mystery, which has an eternal dimension, (hidden in God), and its historical fulfillment (in Christ and the Church). Isaiah's analogy certainly refers to the historical love of God with His chosen people, but these elements are only "in embryo form". The Ephesians fully reveals the mystery. Still, Isaiah helps us to understand Ephesians.   *September 22, 1982*

96. CHRIST'S SPECIAL LOVE –
THE INVISIBLE MADE VISIBLE

Penetrating the Mystery

We can use this analogy of spousal love in Ephesians 5:21-33, to penetrate the mystery of God's loving plan. Although providing only an incomplete understanding of God's plan, the analogy does allow some cognitive penetration into His plan.

Twofold Dimension

It shows that God's love is a total and irrevocable gift of self. There is a two-fold dimension, the individual man and the whole community. Isaiah calls this latter, "Israel" and Ephesians calls it "Church". We could say, "The People of God of the Old and New Covenant".

Although not totally hiding the personal dimension, both writers place this communal meaning in the forefront, using the "person" to stand for "the community". Israel and Church are seen as bride/person.

Three Parts
The analogy allows us to understand that God is Creator and Redeemer as well as the God of the covenant. The analogy has three parts - spousal love, love of compassion (Israel) and paternal love (Ephesians). Each of these analogies contains a part of the mystery.

Total and Radical
Spousal love shows that this gift is total, radical and irrevocable. The totality is limited because man is not able to receive the full gift of God which is "uncreated grace". (The total gift can be shared only by God in the community of the Divine Persons). God gives to man a participation in His divine nature (2Pt.1:4). The gift is total in the sense that this is all God can give to the limited faculties of man. This is the radical character of "created grace".

Christ's Spousal Love
Ephesians radically transforms this analogy of spousal love and leads us to the mystery of grace. This reality was hidden in God and was given to man by Christ. This mystery of Christ redeeming us illumines spousal love and we can learn much about marriage from Christ's spousal love for His Church.

Now A Sign
Secondly, the spousal love analogy helps us approach the question of sacrament. The sacramentality of marriage, (which is justified by Ephesians 5:21-33), presents Christ's relationship to the Church as spousal love. The eternal mystery is fulfilled in Christ and is expressed in the visible order. The mystery is now visible and is present in the "sphere of sign".

Now Made Visible
Sign brings about the "visibility of the invisible". The mystery "hidden in God" has become visible in Christ. Christ's

spousal relationship with His Church, (the "great mystery") provides a concrete visibility.

The indissoluble relationship of Christ/Church is linked with the indissoluble relationship of husband/wife and with God's creative acts in Genesis 2:24, (the institution of marriage). Ephesians tells us that creation is the "visibility of the invisible", the very origin of man's theological history.

Linking the Two Signs

The visible sign of marriage "in the beginning" is linked to the visible sign of Christ and His Church. This brings the eternal plan into history and makes it the foundation of the whole sacramental order. Ephesians has linked these two signs of creation and redemption, making the one great sign, "the great sacrament".

September 29, 1982

97. MARRIAGE – A SIGN OF ELECTION FROM THE BEGINNING

Reviewing the Teachings on Genesis

Man appears in the visible world as the highest expression of God's gift, bearing within himself the "interior dimension" of the gift. He possesses a particular likeness to God by which he dominates and transcends his "visibility", his corporality, his masculinity and femininity and his nakedness. He has a "primordial awareness" of his body's conjugal meaning which is pervaded by original innocence. Man, with his body, is the primordial sacrament which transmits to the visible world the invisible mystery hidden in God. This mystery of man's participation in God's life begins through man's original innocence. This sums up our teachings in Genesis.

Genesis and Ephesians

Because Ephesians quotes the words of Genesis (Eph.5:31-Gen.3:24), we must examine Ephesians in light of our teachings on the "beginning". How can we see in these words (5:21-33) a statement about the primordial sacrament?

Before Creation

Ephesians shows the eternal plan of God which preceded the creation of the world and the creation of man. This plan includes the original innocence of man created as male and female. It also includes the fruit of "being chosen". "He chose us ... that we should be holy and blameless before him" (1:4). This echoes Genesis, "God saw everything that he had made, and behold it was very good." (1:31). Only after sin, did man need to hide himself from the Lord God because he was naked (3:10).

Elected In Christ From the Beginning

Before sin, man enjoyed his eternal election in Christ and man (male and female) was "holy and blameless". This primordial (original) holiness was evident. Both "were naked" but "they were not ashamed" (2:25). Therefore, both Genesis and Ephesians show that man, at creation, was already imbued with his election in Christ, "He destined us to be his sons in Jesus Christ according to the purpose of his will ..." (Eph.1:5-6).

Election In Christ – Even Before Christ

Even though Christ had not yet come to earth or redeemed us in His blood (Eph.1:7) man, male and female, already shared in the gift of Christ's bounty. Only after sin and in spite of sin did the redemption become the source of man's endowment. This endowment came from man's election in Christ, even though that election happened before Christ. By creation, this election happened only to the first Adam who was created in God's image and likeness.

The Body as the Sign of God's Plan

The primordial sacrament of creation is constituted in man, as "body", because only the "body" can make visible what is invisible. Man's body was created to be a sign, transferring into the visible world the mystery hidden from all ages in God.

Holiness and the Primordial Sacrament

Because original innocence was linked to man's experience of his body's conjugal meaning, man saw himself as the subject of holiness. That original holiness belongs to the "sacrament of creation".

The words "A man ... cleaves to his wife and they become one flesh" (2:24) make marriage an integral and central part of this "sacrament of creation", and confirm the character of marriage's origin. Marriage is a sacrament, an integral and central point of the sacrament of creation. In this sense, marriage is the primordial sacrament. *October 6, 1982*

98. MARRIAGE AS A SACRAMENT IS RESTORED BY REDEMPTION

Marriage Remains the "Great Mystery"

Unfortunately, this heritage of grace was driven out when the first covenant with God was broken. Procreation was meant to be illumined by original grace which would be given when God infused the rational soul. This original plan was dimmed by the heritage of original sin and the primordial sacrament of marriage was deprived of its sacramental efficacy. Nevertheless, marriage never ceased being the figure described in Ephesians (5:21-33) as "the great mystery".

Linking the Two Covenants

By quoting the text from Genesis, Ephesians seems to conclude that marriage has remained the "platform for the activation" of God's plans. Marriage connected with grace in original creation, is also part of the "new gracing" in Christ.

Creation had prepared man for redemption and salvation. The analogy of Christ with His Bride shows the definitive renewal of the original grace of the creation covenant.

The Hidden Mystery Fulfilled by Redemption

Ephesians sees this sacrament of redemption as the definitive fulfillment of the mystery hidden from eternity. The author says that in Christ we were "chosen to be holy and blameless" (1:4) and that in Christ "we have redemption in his blood, the remission of sins" (1:7-8).

154

This sacrament of redemption is a new actuation, and in a sense, a new creation. It differs from the original gracing of original innocence because redemption gives man the remission of sins. Yet here, grace abounds even more. "Where sin increased, grace has abounded even more." (Rom.5:21).

Now Permanent and Life-Giving
The sacrament of redemption has become a permanent, life-giving part of the Church. This is the eternal mystery of Christ's self-giving and indissoluble union. The Church completes Christ, just as a wife completes her husband, ("a helper fit for him" - Gen.2:20). From redemption, the Church draws all her spiritual motherhood. "We have been reborn from an incorruptible seed (1Pt.1:23). The visible reality of man/woman destined for marriage becomes, in the sacrament of redemption, the visible reality of the indissoluble union of Christ with His Church.

Visible As A Sign
The "great mystery" is a new actuation of the mystery hidden in God. This visibility refers to marriage (in the sacrament of creation) and the union of Christ with His Church (in the sacrament of redemption). The visibility of the invisible does not totally clear away the mystery. A sacrament is only a sign of an invisible reality.

The Same Mystery
The first Adam (man and woman) was called to conjugal union in the state of innocence and was a sign of the eternal mystery. The "Second Adam" (Christ united with His Church) is the definitive sign of the same mystery. This mystery is now visible through this sacrament which refers to the whole heritage of the sacrament of redemption.   *October 13, 1982*

99.   SACRAMENTS –
POWERS FOR MAN BURDENED BY SIN

Sacraments Emerging From Redemption

The sacramentality of marriage is both a model of the sacrament of the church and an essential part of the new heritage of the sacrament of redemption.

In speaking to the Pharisees (Mt.19:3-9 and Mk.10:5-9), Christ referred only to the original institution of marriage "at the beginning". In the light of Ephesians (5:21-33), we see a two-fold relationship of marriage with the whole sacramental order.

Marriage – The Primordial Sacrament

Marriage, as the primordial sacrament, constitutes the model of God's new plan of salvation and of the sacraments. This sacramental order draws its power from Christ's spousal gift and from His redemption.

The Prototype

Marriage (as the primordial sacrament) is a prototype of the new sacramental order which arises from Christ's redemption. Christ reconfirmed the existence of marriage (Mt.19:3-9) and all the New Testament sacraments find their prototype in marriage.

Marriage does not just have a relationship of "model" with the Church's sacraments. Christ declared that marriage is an integral part of the new order of salvific signs which emerged from redemption. In fact, Christ limited Himself to this unique sacrament of marriage which was instituted in the state of original innocence.

Powers For Man Burdened By Sin

The new sacramental economy is not devoted to a man of innocence but to a man burdened with original sin and the threefold concupiscence (1Jn.2:16). In man, "the desires of the flesh are against the Spirit and the desires of the Spirit are against the flesh" (Gal.5:17).

Moral Norms

Because the new sacramental order has its origins in redemption, marriage must be linked to this new ethos of redemption. Ephesians uses the analogy of marriage for its <u>moral exhortation</u> and explains the moral norms which should guide the Christian.

Clarifying the Word "Sacrament"

In the light of Ephesians (5:21-33), we need to ask questions about the Church's sacraments and clarify the meaning of the term "sacrament", even though this text speaks only in an indirect and secondary way.

Until now, we have been using the word "sacrament" in its biblical, patristic meaning. This is wider than the traditional meaning of "a sign instituted by Christ and administered by the Church which signifies and confers grace on the recipient". According to St. Thomas Aquinas and the scholastic tradition, each sacrament has a definite liturgical matter and form.

"Sacrament" – As Used in Ephesians

Ephesians seemingly authorizes our wider use of the term. The author used "sacrament" to mean God's hidden plan which is now revealed in the sacrament of creation and the sacrament of redemption.

The sacramentality of marriage (the primordial sacrament) is understood within the sacrament of creation. The sacramentality of the Church is understood within the sacramentality of redemption, (which Ephesians presents under the analogy of marriage). Ephesians shows that redemption is a real renewal of the salvific content of creation. These teachings clarify the sacramentality of the Church and of marriage.   *October 20, 1982*

100. REDEMPTION – MAN'S GREAT HOPE

Baptism and Eucharist

The Ephesians text (5:21-33) speaks of Baptism and Eucharist. Christ "loved the Church" and "cleansed her by the washing of water with the word (5:25-26). This washing (Baptism) draws its power from the Redeemer's spousal love. Perhaps the phrase that a man "nourishes and cherishes it (his wife's body), even as Christ does the Church", means the Eucharist (5:29). In Eucharist, Christ nourishes the Church with His own body.

No Developed Theology

Ephesians (5:21-33) does not have a well-developed theology for Baptism, Eucharist, or marriage. The letter focuses on the Church itself as the "great sacrament", the "new sign" of grace whose power is rooted in the sacrament of redemption.

Marriage Realized in New Way

Ephesians declares that marriage (the primordial sacrament) is realized in a new way in Christ and His Church. The spouses are to be "subject to one another" out of reverence for Christ (5:21). Marriage finds its definitive greatness in Christ's spousal relationship with the Church. Although not speaking directly of marriage as a sacrament, Ephesians confirms the sacramentality of marriage within the "great sacrament".

A Review of the Teaching

Because the "great mystery" is Christ's spousal love for His Church, we must review our teaching on "the redemption of the body" (Rom.8:23). Christ's words have a fundamental meaning for every man because he is a "body", and for spouses, united in "one flesh" (Gen.2:24). Christ's words also speak of continence "for the kingdom" (Mt.19:12).

Man's Great Hope

The body's redemption is the great hope of those who possess "the first fruits of the Spirit" (Rom.8:23). In Christ, there is a permanent hope that creation will be "set free from its bondage to decay and obtain the glorious liberty of the children of God" (Rom 8:21).

Christ's words give hope for heavenly life and for daily life. Man possesses "the first fruits of the Spirit. He groans and waits for the redemption of the body." (Rom.8:23) Within this man is that cosmic hope which "waits with eager longing for the revealing of the sons of God" (Rom.8:19).

Christ to the Pharisees

When the Pharisees asked, "Is it lawful to divorce one's wife for any cause?" (Mt.19:3) they mentioned Moses who issued a "bill of divorce" (Dt.24:1), Christ spoke of "the beginning" plan of God, that a man should leave his parents and "cling to his wife as one flesh" (Mt.19:2-6). He set aside Moses' practice of a "bill of divorce", saying that divorce was granted because of "hardness of heart" and "from the beginning it was not so". Christ then declared as "adultery" any marriage involving a divorced man or divorced woman (Mt.19:8-9 and Lk.16:18).

These words (a response to a moral question) open up the horizon of the body's redemption, because they are based on creation which Christ's audience knew well from the book of Genesis.

For Every Man

Christ's words, so decisive for the indissolubility of marriage, are a universal reply. They are given to every historical man who, although deprived of original innocence, does not cease to be male and female, created in God's image. In stressing "the beginning" Christ spoke of the mystery of the redemption of the body. Certainly, Ephesians 5:21-33 can be seen as a witness to the sacramentality of marriage. *October 27, 1982*

101. USING MARRIAGE TO SHOW WHAT IS RESTORED

A Sign of God's Communion of Three Persons

Christ's words to the Pharisees refer to marriage as the primordial revelation of the sacrament of creation. Man and woman are meant to be united in "one flesh", united "in truth and love" as God's children (Gen.2:24). These words are directed to the unity and the communion of the persons (a likeness of God's own inner union). This "unity of the body" continues to mold human history, even though this unity has somewhat lost its full sign.

Restoring the Original Action

Christ confirmed marriage as a sacrament instituted by the Creator, and insisted on its indissolubility. In doing so, Christ opened marriage to the saving graces flowing from the redemption of the body. By redemption, the spouses can overcome sin and re-establish the original unity. This new saving action resumes the original sanctifying action in creation.

A New Ethos (Ethical Norms)

Christ's words on divorce eloquently express ethical norms which are based on the mystery of redemption. This is called the ethos of redemption. Certainly we can discover this ethos through a philosophy based on true personalism (cf. Pope John Paul II's book, "Love and Responsibility").

Our basis is theology and these ethical norms are called the "ethos of the redemption of the body". This ethos helps us to understand the dignity of the human body, the personal dignity of man and woman, and the basis for marriage's indissolubility.

Drawing Ethical Conclusions

Seeing marriage as part of the mystery of redemption, Christ drew the ethical conclusions that divorce and remarriage constitute adultery (Mk.10:11-12). Redemption constitutes a new covenant, and the moral ethos flowing from this redemption must correspond to this new action of God. Marriage, therefore, must be an effective sign of God's saving action, showing that the spouses can consciously participate in the redemption of their bodies.

Creation – Restored to Dignity By Redemption

In describing a man "who looks at a woman lustfully" as having "already committed adultery with her in his heart", Christ delineates this ethical dimension (Mt.5:77-78). Although not directly referring to marriage as a sacrament, these words show the sacramental foundation and refer to individual persons and their original dignity of being in God's image. This dignity has now been restored to man through redemption and is continually "assigned to man" as his duty.

Assigning Moral Duties

By interpreting the commandment, "You shall not commit adultery", Christ assigned a new mode of behavior. This new ethos is the task of every man because of the dignity of every woman, and is the duty of every woman because of the dignity of every man. Christ also assigned duties to every person because of their own dignity and holiness.

This new ethos flows from the redemption of the body, and achieves its full meaning in the sacrament of creation and the sacrament of redemption. In these two mysteries, man can rediscover the holiness of the body's conjugal union.

Given to the Man of Lust

While explaining the mystery of redemption, Christ also spoke of the mystery of man. He spoke of the "heart", that intimate place of good and evil which bears within itself the "interior man of concupiscence of the flesh, of the eyes and of the pride of life" (1Jn.2:16).

A Sign of Redemption

To this man of concupiscence, Christ highlights marriage as a redemptive sign of God's covenant. He assigns an ethos to man's heart, his looks and his behavior. Marriage is a sacrament of creation. Due to man's sinfulness, it is now a part of the sacrament of redemption.   *November 24, 1982*

102. UNDERSTANDING THE FULL POWER OF MARRIAGE

Indissolubility – An Exhortation to Overcome

Marriage is an efficacious expression of God's saving power which accomplishes God's plan in spite of sin and concupiscence. By teaching the indissolubility of marriage, Christ exhorted man to a dominion over concupiscence. This requires a deepened sense of the other person's dignity, both in conjugal life and in other mutual relations.

A Grace With Ethical Norms

St Paul, especially in First Corinthians, (C.7) teaches that marriage is a grace which has a clear system of norms. Although seeing virginity for the kingdom as having "superiority", he states "each has his own gift from God" (7:7). He recommends marriage "because of the temptation to immorality" (7:2) and because "It is better to marry than to be aflame with passion." (7:9).

Marriage is a "remedy for concupiscence", and a grace with an ethos (a system of ethical norms). Paul's verb, "to be aflame" signifies a disorder of the passions coming from concupiscence (cf Sir.23:17). Marriage signifies an "ethical order", where Eros and ethos (the system of norms) mutually penetrate the lives of the spouses.

The Call to Dominate Concupiscence

Because marriage has an indissoluble character, the Spirit exhorts the spouses to draw power from the redemption of their bodies, practicing that chastity "which is proper to them according to the Spirit" (Rom.8:4-5 and Gal. 5:25). Redemption calls them to dominate concupiscence (their tendencies to egoistic gratification). Through the power of the sacrament, marriage can become the basis for a true communion of persons even though it is affected by concupiscence,.

Redeemed Flesh – A Basis for True Communion

The spouses should become one flesh and, through life in the Spirit, can rediscover their spousal gratification. Just as concupiscence darkens the inward vision and deprives the heart of clarity, so life in the Spirit (the grace of the sacrament) helps the spouses to find true liberty and to discover a full awareness of the body's spousal meaning.

Becoming Parents

The Spirit helps the spousal union to share in the blessing of procreation. Eve said, "I have begotten a man with the help of the Lord." (Gen. 4:1).

Due to a profound awareness of the holiness of life, the spouses give thanks when they become parents, because new life is "the first fruits of the Spirit" (Rom.8:23). "The whole creation has been groaning in travail together until now" (8:20). A mother accepts this travail with hope because every newborn child carries a spark of the "revelation of the sons of God" (8:22).

The Hope Springing From Marriage

Within the human heart, this hope struggles with concupiscence which is "not of the Father, but of the world" (1Jn.2:16). Because marriage comes "from the Father" and not "from the world", it constitutes the basis of hope for parents and children. "The world passes away" but the "will of God abides forever" (1Jn.2:17). Man's origin and future (both earthly and heavenly) are connected with marriage.

Marriage – The Carrier of Future Resurrection

Christ spoke of man's earthly and heavenly existence when He said, "the sons of this age marry" but that "those who gain the resurrection of the dead do not" (Lk.20:34-36).

Although marriage does not pertain to the heavenly reality, man has his origin in his parents' marriage and procreation. Although excluding marriage from the heavenly world, Christ shows the need for this sacrament so that men and women can participate in the resurrection.

Marriage does not pertain to the redemption of the body in its heavenly dimension. However, the spouses accept marriage in hopes of heavenly life. Marriage comes "from the Father" and not "from the world which passes". Therefore, marriage contains man's future resurrection, because everyone exists because of the procreative act. Only marriage fulfills the irreplaceable task of providing new human persons called to heavenly life.

December 1, 1982

163

103. THE LINKING OF CREATION AND REDEMPTION

Marriage – At the Beginning and In Christ

Ephesians speaks of the "great mystery" and links marriage to "the beginning". This great mystery (the union of Christ with His Church) is an analogy which helps us to rediscover marriage as both the sacrament "of the beginning" and the fruit of Christ's spousal love.

Spouses must model their union on Christ's union with the Church, ("Husbands, love your wives as Christ loved the Church Eph.5:25). Man and woman are called to participate in God's creative love, the blessing of fruitfulness (Gen.1:28).

Renewing the Marital Structure

The mystery of redemption renews the original structure of marriage. The spouses draw upon God's love. This is revealed in Christ's love for His Church and is renewed when the spouses are united "out of reverence for Christ" (Eph.5:21).

Linking the Two Mysteries

The "great mystery" fuses the redemptive and spousal aspects of love. By grace, these two aspects can permeate the spouses' life. In Ephesians, the original spousal significance of the body (manifested in creation and in original innocence) is linked to its redemptive significance. The body is "newly created".

This linking helps us to understand marriage and the meaning of "being a body" (man and woman). The "great mystery" demands that we link the spousal meaning with the redemptive meaning of the body. Only in this way, do the spouses find the meaning of "being a body".

A New Form in Celibacy

This "great mystery" (of Christ's special love for His Church) spoke indirectly of celibacy for the kingdom. In celibacy, the linking of the spousal and redemptive meaning takes a different form. For those who have embraced this state, Christ's giving of Himself for the Church is the fullest incarnation of the ideal of celibacy. In this way, the mystery of redemption bears fruit in a special way.

The Mystery Speaks to All
Although addressed to spouses, Ephesians speaks to everyone and to all history. Christ's love for the Church is the new sacrament "of man and of the world". Just as the creation of man was the original sacrament, so redemption is the new sacrament (into which marriage is inserted).

Seeing the Meaning of Human Existence
If man sees creation in the light of redemption, then the meaning of human existence will be revealed. The body's spousal meaning is completed only by the redemptive meaning. The body's meaning is not limited to marriage or virginity but is found in diverse situations, such as human suffering and in the very birth and death of man.

By means of the New Covenant, marriage is again inscribed in the "sacrament of man". Redemption releases forces by which this "sacrament of man" brings about the fulfillment of God's Kingdom, for marriage is a vivifying part of God's saving process.   *December 15, 1982*

104. EXAMINING THE MARRIAGE VOWS

A Public Vow
At their wedding, the engaged couple says, "I take you as my wife" and "I take you as my husband". They promise to be faithful to one another "in joy and in sorrow, in sickness and in health, and to love and honor (each other) all the days of their life".

By these words, the couple minister the sacrament to one another, in the presence of the priest and many witnesses, (two of whom act officially). Therefore, marriage is a public act by which man and woman become husband and wife before the Church.

Completed by the Conjugal Act
These sacramental words are the sign of a "marriage coming into being". This is distinguished from the consummation

of the marriage. A non-consummated marriage has not yet been fully constituted as a marriage. The words "I take you" are fulfilled only by conjugal intercourse, which was determined by God "from the beginning" as a becoming "one flesh" (Gen.2:27).

By their words, the spouses show a willingness to have conjugal relations. Both the words and the conjugal relations are part of the sacramental sign to which we will devote these reflections.

Examining the Words

The sacrament is constructed by these words which show "who" the couple intends to be from now on, that is, "living for each other". These words are vital both for what they say and with what they determine.

The words constitute the sacramental sign because the "reality" of their bodies corresponds to the words. The couple, as ministers of the sacrament, are the sacrament's full visible sign. The words constitute the sacramental sign only because they correspond to the couple's masculinity and femininity (just as it was "in the beginning"). By the language of their bodies they are a reciprocal gift in the conjugal union.

Expressing An Intention

These spoken words have a unique, intentional expression, ("I take you as my wife/husband"). They also show a communion of persons "always faithful in joy and in sorrow, in sickness or in health ... all the days of my life". This enduring and ever new language of the body becomes the constitutive element of the communion of persons, a reciprocal gift in their masculinity and femininity.

Conferring A New Aspect

The spouses' words confer on each other a new aspect of their personal and interpersonal lives. Their words recall the perennial language of the body as an unrepeatable sign which has meaning for their entire future. This is a visible sign of God's covenant in Christ as each has "their own special gift" (1Cor.7:7).

Civil Law and Theology

According to civil law, the newlyweds enter into a well-defined conjugal pact by which they have become socially recognized as spouses. This human reality of marriage also has many religious-moral aspects. Marriage is based upon the covenant of man with God in Christ and has received a new origin in redemption "the union of the sons of God in truth and in love" (GS 24). The liturgy gives a form to this sign which the spouses must hear throughout their lives.   *January 5, 1983*

Part Eight
Important Texts From the Old Testament

105. THE PROPHETS REVEAL THE MYSTERY

Prophetism of the Body

The long biblical tradition affirms that the language of the body enters into the structure of marriage as a sacramental sign. The prophets (especially Hosea, Ezekiel and Deutero-Isaiah) prepare for the classical Ephesian text which proclaims a new covenant under the form of the marriage of Christ with His Church. We can call this tradition "the prophetism of the body".

The Objective Level – The Covenant

The analogy has two levels. First, the prophets see the "covenant" as a marriage of God with Israel. This comes directly from God's initiative, first with Abraham and then with Moses. This marital relationship has a personal bonding which deepens this "pact". Isaiah (54:10) states "my steadfast love shall not depart from you".

The Subjective Level – The Spousal Meaning

In calling God "Lord of the covenant" and "Father of Israel", the prophets show the absolute dominion of Yahweh over Israel (the spousal dimension). Therefore, Israel's sins are not just a breaking of a pact. They are an infidelity and a betrayal, piercing the heart of the Spouse.

This spousal relationship reveals the second level of the analogy, the language of the body. The prophets compare the covenant to marriage, (the objective sense), and then pass quickly to the subjective sense, the spousal meaning of the body in its masculinity and femininity. This is the language of "fidelity" or of "infidelity".

The Prophets

Hosea called worship of other gods the "adultery" of Israel. He condemned this adultery in words and in prophetic signs. He followed God's command "Go, take to yourself a wife of harlotry

168

and have children of harlotry, for the land commits great harlotry by forsaking the Lord" (1:12). In this act, Hosea shows that Yahweh is a sensitive, affectionate Spouse. He is also severe, because His fidelity contrasted sharply with the actions of the unfaithful Israel.

Ezekiel speaks of the adultery of Jerusalem and Samaria, "I plighted my troth to you and entered into a covenant with you and you became mine." (16:8).

A Language of the Body

For the prophets, the body "speaks a language". This shows man's call to a union of persons, which can be expressed only by the body. The most profound words of man's spirit demand an adequate language of the body, which refers either to marriage or to man's celibacy for the kingdom.

A Glimpse of the Covenant

The prophets express Yahweh's relationship to Israel through spousal love. They praise fidelity and condemn infidelity as adultery. In this way, they establish more than just the moral and ethical categories of truth and falsehood. Their words reveal a glimpse of Yahweh's covenant, where truth is fidelity and falsehood is adultery.

This goes beyond logic. When Israel acts in accord with the spousal meaning of the body, it is truth. When Israel contradicts this spousal significance, it is falsehood.

January 12, 1983

106. THE MARRIAGE VOWS AND THE PROPHETS' LANGUAGE

The Spouses and the Prophets

The language of the male and female body is part of the integral structure of the sacramental sign. This is expressed by the words, "I take you as my wife ... as my husband" and is the "essential truth" of the body which must exclude any "non-truth".

Fidelity speaks "truth" and non-fidelity speaks "non-truth". By these words, the newlyweds follow the prophets' teachings because the visible sign of the covenant goes back "to the beginning" and is sustained by redemption.

Accepting the Body's Language

The prophets say that the body has a language which the spouses must accept. The body, as masculine and feminine, is a personal subject. When the newlywed couple proclaim this truth as the principle of their new life together, they perform a prophetic act and participate in the Church's prophetic mission. They express in human words the truth which comes from God.

Many Parts to Their Vows

This prophetic proclamation is complex. First, the vows announce and bring about the fact that they will be husband and wife. Their reciprocal profession is made before God. The vows of consent speak clearly of "I" and "you", constituting the union-communion of the persons. The consent is prophetic. It proclaims a truth which comes from God and is spoken in His name.

Speaking a Biblical Language

God established this language by creating man as male and female. This language carries the richness of creation and redemption, and is expressed by the couple in their vows. Before being spoken by the spouses, these words were spoken by God (in Genesis, in the prophets, and in the Ephesians).

"The language of the body" is the language inscribed in the male and female body, and is spoken afresh by the spouses. Their marriage vows take on a prophetic character and the spouses bring about a visible sign of the Church. Their vows contain an intention, a decision, and a choice, namely, to act in conformity with this language of their bodies. The spouses profess that they want their behavior to be in conformity with the language that God inscribed in their bodies.

The Future Results

The spouses give clear meaning to their actions and, by their vows, they constitute the matrimonial sign. This consent will produce (in the future) the lasting results of an indissoluble marriage, "all the days of my life". Fulfilling this matrimonial sign is closely linked to the morality of matrimonial conduct. This must include procreation and the future gift of paternity/maternity. They have responded "yes" to the question, "Will you accept children lovingly from God and bring them up according to the law of Christ and His Church?" *January 19, 1983*

107. THE SPOUSES SPEAK LIKE PROPHETS

Prophetism of the Body

Whenever a couple exchanges consent, a marriage is constituted. This is according to God's design "from the beginning" and is based on Christ's special love for His Church. This consent is according to the language of the body. Although the body does not "speak", the spouses make their vows according to the truths inscribed in their bodies, their masculinity and femininity.

Man, male and female, permits the body to speak "for him" and "in his name". This is a "prophetism of the body" because the body speaks on the authority of the person.

Speaking for Years to Come

The wedding vows (the initial sign of the sacrament) are continually completed by this "prophetism of the body". By actions and gestures of tenderness, their bodies will speak throughout the years of marriage and will carry out the "conjugal dialogue".

This dialogue must be done "in truth", for the spouses must form a communion of persons. By their conduct and actions, the spouses must "author" those meanings which correspond to language of the body. Love, fidelity, conjugal uprightness and a union lasting until death must be continually built and deepened.

Living in Truth

These meanings of marriage are "programmed" into the conjugal consent, so that the spouses might live them in truth. An organic bond exists between the language of the body, (given in matrimonial consent), and the use of the language in the subsequent years of marriage.

This language must correspond to the truth of the body. This is the "prophetism of the body". If the spouses confer this truth on all the spheres of their married life, they will live "in the truth". If not, they are guilty of a lie, falsifying the language of the body.

The Spouses as Prophets

By marriage, the spouses can participate in the Church's prophetic mission. Those spouses who use the language of the body correctly, for special and creative love, are true prophets and show the full grandeur of conjugal consent.

Even though constructed on a theology, marriage's sacramental sign teaches us about human nature. Christ's words about lust and concupiscence open the doors to many insights about human nature. Even though burdened by sin and concupiscence, man and woman are still invited to enter into redemption and be sharers in a sacrament of grace. *January 26, 1983*

108. THE BATTLE BETWEEN CONCUPISCENCE AND REDEMPTION

The Effects of Lust

Besides teaching the unity and indissolubility of marriage, Christ also said, "You shall not commit adultery" and "Everyone who looks at a woman lustfully has already committed adultery with her in his heart." (Mt.5:28).

The man of concupiscence will not correctly read this language of the body and will not express that language in a marriage which should be a lasting pact. The Old Testament prophets called Israelite idolatry "the adultery of Israel and Judah".

Jesus understood "adultery" more deeply than the prophets and called men away from their concupiscence. His teaching is quite different from contemporary thinkers, those "masters of suspicion" who see man as helplessly ensnarled in his lusts.

The Power of Concupiscence

Although graced by the sacrament and by his own marital consent, man is still a "man of concupiscence". At the same time, man can experience the redemption of the body. This power is in every man and contains a set of ethical norms for the human person.

Concupiscence does not destroy the capacity of the person to give marriage vows or to live up to those vows. Concupiscence does cause many errors and gives rise to sin (whether conjugal or extra-conjugal). Nevertheless, the redemption of the body offers every man the possibility of going from error to truth and from sin to chastity.

The Christian Possibilities

By living according to the Christian understanding of the body's language, man becomes the enduring sign of conjugal love. By fidelity "in joy and in sorrow, in sickness and in health", man expresses the body's language in a family communion of persons. The man of concupiscence becomes a new reality of redemption.

A Capable Co-Author

The sacramental sign of marriage gives a specific theological understanding of man. He is a subject capable of self-determination and can become a sign of creation and redemption. Being burdened by concupiscence does not limit man's capacity to understand the language of the body and to distinguish truth from falsehood. Every man authors the meaning of his own life, whether in truth or falsehood.

Called and Not Accused

The libido does not determine man. Otherwise, his behavior (even the choice of continence for the kingdom) would be merely a transformation of his libido. Man alone is a true author of the language of his body, whether that language is true or false. He must not be condemned to suspect himself. A libido overwhelmed by concupiscence can only accuse man. It cannot call him to truth.

The sacrament says clearly that man is really called, not accused, even though he is a man of concupiscence.

February 9, 1983

109. THE RICH DESCRIPTIONS OF SPOUSAL LOVE IN THE SONG OF SONGS

The Body as Visible Sign

The Song of Songs has sometimes been discouraged as "profane" and, at other times, has become the source of mystical writings. We place this book outside the sphere of the great prophetic analogy (Yahweh's special love for Israel), but we do connect its teachings with the primordial sacrament in Genesis. The Song of Songs is certainly part of the biblical stream and provides a richness of language in which the human body is the visible sign of the covenant.

The Richness of the Genesis "Discovery"

In the Song of Songs, the spouses move in a circle formed by love. Their words and gestures show the inner movement of their hearts and express the language of the body. In this, there is a discovery of "a helper like himself", taken from his side (Gen.2:20).

The Song of Songs gives this "discovery" a richness of human language. It develops the simple description of the man's thoughts in Genesis into a full dialogue between the spouses. It also reflects the wonder and admiration expressed by the first man upon seeing the first woman.

Focus on the Body

The poem's point of departure and of arrival is the mutual fascination which arises from the direct experiencing of the bride's femininity and the groom's masculinity. This concentration upon the body, the source of mutual fascination and of the direct attraction, generates love as an interior impulse.

This love unleashes a special experience of the "beautiful", which involves the entire person and gives rise to mutual satisfaction. "O most beautiful among women" (1:8) says the groom. These words of a spellbound man are repeated in all five stanzas, and are echoed also by the bride. "I am dark ... but lovely, O daughters of Jerusalem" (1:5).

174

A Language of Metaphors

These metaphors are borrowed from both the life of shepherds and from the royal status of the groom. Using these metaphors shows that the language of the body must be corroborated by the whole visible world.

The heart and eyes of the groom concentrate totally on the female "I", which is expressed through every feminine trait. This gives rise to his total enchantment. The female "I" speaks little, but finds a rich echo in the words of the groom who expresses his experiences of beauty and of love.

While these metaphors use analogies with visible things, they also indicate the insufficiency of these images. The groom addressing himself to the bride (whose body alone can express full femininity) ends his song saying, "You are all beautiful, my beloved, and there is no blemish in you" (4:3).

May 23, 1984

110. SONG OF SONG IMAGES – BELOVED, SISTER, ENCLOSED GARDEN AND FOUNTAIN SEALED

A Descriptive Theology

In expressing the bride's values, the groom says, "You have ravished my heart with one glance of your eyes, with one bead of your necklace. How sweet are your caresses, my sister, my bride." (4:9-10). These words show the theology of the sacramental sign of marriage, namely, to know who the female "you" is for the male "I", and vice-versa.

Beloved and Sister

The groom exclaims "You are all beautiful my beloved" (4:7) and calls her "my sister, my bride" (4:9). "Sister" is more eloquent that "beloved" and shows how love reveals the other person.

"Beloved", (always essential to love), places the second "I" beside one's own "I" and reveals an inner unifying power. However, being both "sister and bride" has a special eloquence. There is a union between the two and yet there is a difference which comes from her feminine originality.

175

"Sister" speaks not just of "sex", but of person, a female person in relationship to a man. It speaks of her openness to the man who is perceived as a "brother". "Sister" helps identify the man and challenges him to see himself as "brother".

"Sister" – A Common Belonging

The groom accepts this challenge and seeks their common past, as if he and his bride were united from infancy. They feel as close as a brother and sister who came from the same mother. This "common belonging" allows them to love their mutual closeness in security. They do not fear any unfair judgment of other men.

By saying "sister", the groom reproduces those stages of her life when she was loved as a feminine person, when she was in her girlhood and tenderly loved. Hence, the bride is filled with a bodily peace which resembles sleep. "Do not arouse, do not stir up love before its time". The peace of this encounter lies in their reciprocal, disinterested love. "So am I in your eyes, like one who has found peace." (8:10)

Images of Self-Possession

Another plot emerges in the groom's words, "You are an enclosed garden, my sister, my bride, an enclosed garden, a fountain sealed" (4:12).

An "enclosed garden" and "a fountain sealed" show the personal dignity of the woman who is master of her own mystery. As spiritual subject, she possesses her own authentic gift and yet she is inclined to the spousal union described in Genesis.

Images of True Love

"The sister bride", "the enclosed garden" and "the fountain sealed" show the inner inviolability of the person and the authentic depth of the mutual belonging of the spouses. They are aware of their destiny for each other, "My lover belongs to me and I to him." (2:16).

There is the nuptial meaning of femininity in relation to the groom, who speaks of his bride as a "garden enclosed" and a "fountain sealed". The bride freely entrusts herself, "I belong to

176

my lover". The bride's freedom of the gift corresponds to the groom's awareness of the gift. This leads to authentic love.

May 30, 1984

111. SONG OF SONGS - DESCRIBING THE PERSONAL SEARCHING AND BELONGING

Nearness

The Song of Songs expresses the language of the body as it describes the spouses' progressive approach which increases their love. Nearness means entering into the mystery of the other person without violating it.

The increasing nearness comes through the heart's affections so that the one person "can taste" the other. "His fruit is sweet to my mouth." (2:3).

Longing and Giving

The groom describes the bride's beauty, her feet, thighs, navel, body, breasts, neck, eyes, nose, head and hair (7:1-8) as a gift from a self-giving person.

The bride, knowing his longing, gives herself quickly in a love that is spiritual and sensual, "I belong to my lover and for me he yearns." (7:11). Together, their mutual love seals their whole life.

Solitude – Rediscovery - Search

This language of the body becomes part of a mutual attraction, which is often expressed in a nostalgia of affectionate solitude, ("Do not arouse, do not stir up love before its own time") and of mutual rediscovery, ("I was sleeping, but my heart kept vigil; I heard my lover knocking.").

Their joy leads them on a continual search. In their reaching and experiencing one another, they ceaselessly tend toward something. They yield to the gift which dominates the moment and surpasses "Eros". This search for integral beauty has an inner dimension in which the heart is awake even in sleep (5:2).

A Restlessness

The Song of Songs shows a human Eros whose restlessness is evident. "I sought him but I did not find him. I called to him but he did not answer me." (5:6) The energies of human desires are at work within a person who is fully aware of a faithful and exclusive belonging.

Other parts of the poem show the cause of the search and the restlessness. This accompanies their awareness of mutual belonging, and shows the need for self-control. The personal awareness demands a search which will bring about their mutual belonging.

Beyond the Expressions of Belonging

This inner dynamic of love shows that a person cannot be totally dominated, because the human person surpasses all measure of possession and gratification. Therefore, the spouses realize that their belonging is really a "mutual gift" and love is "as stern as death", exceeding even the language of the mortal body. This truth calls the spouses beyond the expressions of mutual belonging so they can arrive at the heart of their reciprocal gift.

Compared to "Love" in St. Paul

The poem approaches St Paul's teaching in which Eros is integrated into a higher truth. "Love is patient. Love is kind. Love is not jealous. Love is never rude or self-seeking. There is no limit to love's forbearance, to its trust, its hope, its power to endure. Love never fails." (1Cor.13:4-8).

A Completion of Eros

The Song of Songs says that love's "jealousy" is "restless as the nether world" (8:6) but Paul says that "love is not jealous". What is the relationship between a love that is "stern as death" and a love that "never fails"?

New Testament love has new unsuspected perspectives. While human Eros has a "closed horizon", Paul's love has an "open horizon" which emerges from the person and calls him to a personal communion. This is agape love, which completes "Eros" by purifying it. *June 6, 1984*

112. THE MARRIAGE LOVE OF TOBIAH AND SARAH

In describing the wedding of Tobiah and Sarah, the Book of Tobit uses the expression "sister" (noting a fraternal quality in spousal love) and also says "his heart became set on her" (6:19). The Song of Songs had said that love is "as stern as death".

Facing Real Death

Sarah, daughter of Raguel, had "already been married seven times " (6:14) and all of her husbands died before having conjugal relations. Tobiah had reasons to fear because this was the work of a demon.

Therefore, from the very beginning, Tobiah's love faced the reality of death, and the words, "love is as stern as death" are a real test for these spouses. However, they unhesitatingly accept the challenge and overcome the demon of death on their wedding night.

Between Good and Evil

The story shows a young couple caught in the middle of the powers of good and evil. This struggle between good and evil is completely missing in the Song of Songs, which describes an ideal and abstract world as though this struggle did not exist. In truth, only the interior power of love overcomes the struggles that take place within and outside the person.

Human life places every man between the forces of good and evil (both within and around him), but the power of love gives him a confidence that he will do everything that is needed to overcome. The love of Tobiah and Sarah does not use the rapturous language of the Song of Songs, but their choices and actions confront the real burdens of human existence. By the language of their body, they use the words of choice and overcome by prayer.

A Prayer of Tobiah

Tobiah's prayer (8:5-8), filled with praise, thanksgiving and supplication, makes the language of the body an "objectified language", not so much filled with emotion but with a true understanding of the gravity of his experience.

The spouses come before the God of the covenant, the "God of our fathers". (This is the language of spouses as the ministers of the sacrament.) They are aware that their conjugal pact originated with creation and is an image of the original sacrament.

Their final words, "Call down your mercy on me and on her and allow us to live together to a happy old age." (8:7) show their desire of preserving their union until death. Although they face death on their wedding night, they see that God is still calling them to conjugal union and ask, "Call down your mercy on me and her"

Two Parts of the Sign

While the couple in the Song of Songs declare their human love, Tobiah and Sarah ask God's help in their love. Both are part of marriage's sacramental sign. These are the subjective aspect of the human heart and the objective aspect of a union lived in truth. The prayer of the newlyweds confirms the Song of Songs in a deeply moving way. *June 27, 1984*

113. THE MYSTICAL LANGUAGE OF THE LITURGY

Marriage – Lifted Up Into the Mystical

We return to Ephesians (5:21-23) and the mystical aspect of the body's language. "The great mystery" (5:32), is fulfilled in Christ's spousal relationship with His Church and is definitively carried out in heaven. Ephesians, however, extends this mystical meaning to the marriage between man and woman who "defer to one another out of reverence for Christ" (5:21).

Fulfilled In Mystery

This radically frees our thinking from Manicheaism (that the body is evil) or from considering the body in a non-personal way. This mystical meaning brings the language of the body closer to real holiness. The sacraments inject this holiness into God's plan for humanity, penetrating the body and the soul with God's power. The liturgy expresses all of these ideas, as it elevates the conjugal pact to the realm of mystery and enables it to be fulfilled in mystery.

180

An Array of Responsibilities

The liturgical words express an interpersonal event which the couple will maintain "until death". The sacrament includes both the words of consent and the living out of that consent. The couple will have these tasks of love, fidelity and conjugal honesty until death. They must preserve their own holiness and the holiness of their life together. The liturgical language shows the complete array of marital responsibilities, those duties which form the spirituality of marriage.

This liturgical language (which is truly the language of the body) is like the Song of Songs in expressing the attraction and mutual pleasure. It is also like the Ephesians and shows the holiness of the person in the mystery of creation of man, male and female.

A Review of Scriptural Texts

The reverence for Christ and for each other which is required by Ephesians is a spiritually mature form of the mutual attraction revealed in Genesis (2:23-25) and which flows through the Song of Songs and Tobit.

This spiritual maturity is the blossoming of "piety", the gift of fear from the Holy Spirit (1Thes.4:4-7) and is a charismatic gift of "life according to the Spirit" (Rom.8:5).

Ephesians says the virtue is practiced "out of reverence for Christ". By the Spirit's gift and the person's virtue, the mutual attraction becomes spiritually mature, leading the spouses away from concupiscence and into a true "freedom of the gift".

Living the Vows

Only by living out their vows can the spouses make their wedding promises the language of their own bodies in a beauty not known before. Through the liturgical language, the spouses encounter the "great mystery". They must transfer these liturgical words into the language of their own bodies by a fidelity and a conjugal honesty, which is rooted in the redemption of the body (Rom.8:23). In this way, they live the liturgy through their conjugal life. *July 4, 1984*

Part Nine
Reflections on the Encyclical "Humanae Vitae"

114. THE TWO MEANINGS AND THEIR INSEPARABLE CONNECTION

Applying the Principles to Moral Questions

Because the reflections in the previous chapters must be applied to the moral questions surrounding marriage and the family, we will examine the encyclical, Humanae Vitae (On Human Life) in light of these principles.

Humanae Vitae (HV) says, "The Church teaches as absolutely required that in any use whatever of marriage, there must be no impairment of its natural capacity to procreate human life." (11) and "This particular doctrine, often expounded by the Magesterium of the Church, is based on the inseparable connection, established by God, which man on his own initiative may not break, between the unitive and procreative significance which are both inherent to the marriage act." (12)

Of Central Importance

This passage has central importance, dealing with the "two significances of the marriage act" and their "inseparable connection". This passage is closely related to marriage as a sacramental sign. It is a central passage, an important part of the whole document and the key to all the components of the entire text.

A True Language

The sacramental sign of marriage is based on the true language of the body, and is affirmed by the newly-weds when they promise to "always be faithful and to love and honor each other all the days of their life." This truth must be reaffirmed throughout their marriage.

The encyclical focuses on the conjugal act when the spouses become "one flesh". This moment is rich in significance, and must be done "in truth" so that the couple acts according to the true value of the body.

182

The Fundamental Structure

Pope Paul VI explains the reasons for this "inseparable connection". "The reason is that the marriage act, because of its fundamental structure, while it unites husband and wife in the closest intimacy, also brings into operation laws written into the actual nature of man and of woman for the generation of new life" (12).

These sentences show the meaning and structure of marital relations. They refer to "laws written into the actual nature of a man and a woman". The foundation for this moral norm lies in the nature of this act and, even more deeply, in the very nature of the man and the woman.

The Two Meanings

The fundamental structure of the marriage act is the needed foundation in discovering the two meanings (to unite and to procreate). Both these meanings must be part of the conscious decision of the couple. Both union and procreation happen because of "the fundamental structure" of the conjugal act. Spouses must understand this two-fold meaning and not separate them.

The Church bases its moral norm on this truth of the body, which is both real (the structure of the act) and psychological (the subjective decision). *July 11, 1984*

115. A NORM OF NATURAL LAW, SCRIPTURE AND CHURCH TEACHING

Objective and Subjective Reality

Humanae Vitae teaches the objective reality, ("There must be no impairment of the natural capacity to procreate human life.") and also stresses the subjective aspects, ("the two purposes of the marital act"). Because the very structure of the act reveals these two purposes, the letter states clearly that the modern world is able to see "that this teaching is in harmony with human reason" (12).

This reasonable character of the teaching depends on a correct understanding of the intimate nature of the marital act. Knowing the meaning of the act's structure (the inseparable connection between the union of their bodies and the procreation of new life) leads to a moral norm which corresponds to the language of the body.

Based Upon Scripture and Tradition

Humanae Vitae is morally binding. Acting according to this norm is morally right and acting against this norm is morally wrong. Although not taught formally in Scripture, the Church believes She has the teaching authority to interpret natural moral law.

Even if Scripture does not literally contain this moral law (as formulated in Humanae Vitae), this teaching has "often been expounded by the Church's teaching authority"(12). This norm is in accord with the sum total of revealed doctrine in the Scriptures.

A Conformity of Teachings

In the fuller context, this teaching belongs both to the natural order and to the moral order revealed by God. Church tradition, the Magisterium and the encyclical must agree on such truths.

Besides the harmony of this teaching with human reason, there is also a profound conformity with tradition and the biblical view of man. This is the theology of the body and is the basis for moral doctrine.

Because this norm is based upon natural law, it affects everyone. It enlightens especially those believers who find support in the theology of the body. This norm's deeper source lies in the ethical teachings of the Gospel and in the Spirit's actions.

July 18, 1984

116. THE ENCYCLICAL'S PASTORAL APPROACH TO THE PRACTICAL DIFFICULTY

A Completion of the Council's Teaching

This encyclical is based upon the Council's document "On the Modern World" (Gaudium et Spes), and completes its teaching, concerning the "harmony of human love with respect for life". The Council stated that a true contradiction cannot exist between the divine laws pertaining to the transmission of life, and those pertaining to the fostering of authentic conjugal love (GS 51).

Although the encyclical concentrates more on the "inseparable connection" of the two meanings rather than the "non-contradiction", Pope Paul VI does shed light on this "non-contradiction".

A Pastoral Approach

Both the Council teaching (GS) and the encyclical are pastoral documents which confront modern questions in the demographic, socioeconomic and political orders. Pope Paul VI says, "Would it not be right to review the moral norms" since many feel they can be kept "only with the greatest difficulty, sometimes only by heroic effort". (3)

The Pope answers these pastoral questions with a sensitive and profound response. He gives much weight to pastoral arguments, which touch directly the lives of those who must live out these norms.

Pastoral Sensitivity

This sensitivity becomes evident when he writes that, although he is promulgating God's law, yet many will find this difficult or even impossible. Certainly, this law requires a great endurance, made possible only by God's help. This patience enhances the person's dignity and benefits society (20).

Pope Paul focuses on "the possibility of observing the divine law". He senses that an ability to observe the law would show that the norm is not a contradiction and that putting the norm into practice belongs to the pastoral sphere.

Need For True Principles

The theology of the body confirms indirectly the norms of Humanae Vitae. The answers given by Christ to his hearers, and by St. Paul in his small manual on the Christian's moral life, (First Corinthians), provide the principles for the theology of the body and the understanding needed to resolve these problems.

Many overlook the pastoral concern which led to the Council's teaching and to Humanae Vitae. This concern always searched for man's true good and for a promoting of values engraved by God in man's nature. This pastoral concern is faithful to a discovery of God's true plan for human love.

Because of this concern, the Council noted "the harmony of human love with respect for life" (GS 51) and the encyclical is concerned that people can observe the divine law. *July 25, 1984*

117. RESPONSIBLE PARENTHOOD

Concerning responsible parenthood, the Council recalls the basic premises for the Church's teaching. The encyclical goes even further and provides more concrete content.

The Council's Objective Standards

The Council teaches that in harmonizing conjugal love with the responsible transmission of life, the moral norms do not depend solely on the sincere intentions of the couple or an evaluation of their motives. Moral norms must be judged by objective standards, based on the nature of the human person and his acts.

These standards must preserve both the mutual self-giving and human procreation. This is achieved only by the practice of conjugal chastity (GS 51). The Council adds that Catholics cannot use methods of birth control which the Church finds blameworthy (GS 51).

Basis For Their Decision

The Council also asks the couple to make their decisions "by common counsel and effort" with "docile reverence towards God" (GS 50). They must consider "their own welfare and that of their children, those already born and those which the future may bring".

They need to consider "the material and spiritual conditions of the times", "their state in life" and "the interests of the family group, of temporal society and of the Church herself" (GS 50). Only "the parents themselves and no one else should ultimately make this judgment in the sight of God" (GS 50).

Forming the Conscience

The Council says that the spouses cannot "proceed arbitrarily". Their conscience must be "dutifully conformed" to divine law, and "submissive towards the Church's teaching office which authentically interprets that law in the light of the gospels" (GS 50).

The Council establishes unambiguously the basic premises and clarifies the elements of responsible parenthood. The person's mature judgment must be made by a conscience in conformity with the divine law as authentically interpreted by the Church.

Pope Paul – The Total Concept of Man

In his encyclical, Pope Paul VI goes even further than the Council. He excludes beforehand any reduction to the "partial aspects" of this question (as is done by birth control advocates). He is guided by a total concept of man (7) and of conjugal love (8, 9).

Concerning the biological aspects, he says that responsible parenthood demands knowledge of the body's "specific functions". Human intelligence can discover, in the procreation faculties, those biological laws which involve the "human personality". By examining these emotions of man, "responsible parenthood expresses the domination which reason and will must exert over these emotions" (10).

Two Groups of Parents

The Pope teaches that there are two groups of parents who "exercise responsible parenthood". The first group "prudently and generously decide to have a large family." The second group "for serious reasons and with due respect for the moral law", "choose to have no more children for the time being or even for an indeterminate period" (10).

Responsible parenthood requires both a disposition to limit births and to increase the family size in accord with prudence. Parents must examine "the objective moral order instituted by God", which is truly interpreted by a right conscience (HV 10).

Guided by the Inseparable Connection

The couple cannot act arbitrarily, but must be guided by "the intimate structure of the conjugal act" and the "inseparable connection" between the unitive and procreative meaning.

August 1, 1984

118. THE POPE'S CLEAR TEACHING ON METHODS

Illicit and Licit Methods

The Pope clearly distinguishes between a morally licit method and a morally illicit method of birth regulation (more precisely, the regulation of fertility).

Three Illicit Methods

The first illicit method is abortion, which the Pope defines as "the direct interruption of the generative process already begun" (14). A second illicit method is "direct sterilization". Finally, the Pope defines as illicit, "any action, which either before, at the moment of, or after sexual intercourse is specifically intended to prevent procreation" (14). This covers all contraceptive means.

Licit Method

To have "recourse to the infertile periods" is morally licit because "married people may take advantage of the natural cycles immanent in the reproductive system". By having relations "at precisely those times which are infertile" the couple "controls birth without offending moral principles" (16).

Correct and Incorrect Use

The Pope stresses the essential difference between the licit and illicit means. By the licit method, the couples "rightly use a facility provided them by nature". By the illicit method, the couples "obstruct the natural development of the generative process" (16).

The correct use of the fertile period and the incorrect use of artificial contraceptives are ethically distinct. They differ in their intrinsic moral character. Although the married couples using contraception might have "acceptable reasons" for their actions, this does not change the morality of contraception. There is a separate ethical problem when married couples use the natural regulation of fertility without valid reasons.

Normative and Pastoral Dimensions

Couples, even with valid reasons to limit fertility, must respect the intrinsic moral qualities of the marital act. The natural regulation respects this integrity of the act, while "artificial contraception" does not. The Pope gives the normative dimension, (making clear the moral principles involved) and he also gives the pastoral dimension (speaking of "the possibility of observance of the divine law") (20).

The Pope's encyclical shows the normative pastoral aspects of the theology of the body and the true dignity of man and woman in the important questions of the transmission of life. This theology is not just theory but demands that man model his earthly life in hope of a future world. The Pope shows the true good of the person.   *August 8, 1984*

119. USING ARTIFICIAL MEANS DESTROYS THE TRUTH

The Artificial Domination by Technology

The Church's doctrine on the transmission of life maintains an adequate relationship between the "domination of the forces of nature" (technology) and "the mastery of self" (indispensable for the human person). Modern man "has made tremendous progress in the domination of the forces of nature (technology) and endeavors to extend this control over every aspect of his own life, even over the laws that regulate the transmission of life" (2).

Destroying the Human Person

This domination by technology menaces the human person because "mastery of self" is the "natural method", (in accord with the person). Those using artificial means destroy the very constitution of the person, robbing man of his proper subjectivity and making him an object of manipulation.

189

Expressing the Truth

The human body is not just an organism of sexual reactions, but is the means of expressing the total person. The language of the body has an interpersonal meaning, (especially in the man-woman relationship). Sexual relations must express this truth of the sacrament of creation because it reflects God's eternal plan of love. The encyclical describes the practical and pastoral consequences of that truth.

The spouses, in their personal subjectivity, come under the natural law because, as male and female, they witness to and interpret God's plan. By their marital consent (completed by conjugal union), man and woman express the full truth of their bodies. By their gestures and actions, and their sexual dynamism, each "person" speaks.

The Language of Creation

This dialogue began when Adam saw Eve (Gen.2: 24-25) and the language of the body was given on the day of creation. This sexual language is subject to truth and to objective moral norms. Man and woman must express themselves in their fullest dimension, in the whole truth of their human person, masculine and feminine.

Man can give himself as a person only if he is master of self. Self-control is needed for the liberty of the gift. In this communion of persons, the bodily giving is judged by truth.

Separating by Artificial Means

The conjugal act must signify both love and potential fecundity. It cannot be deprived of these meanings by artificial means. Separating love and potential fecundity violates the ultimate truth of the act, because the two are meant to activate each other (12). The conjugal act, deprived of its procreative capacity, ceases to be an act of love.

With artificial contraception, the bodily union does not correspond to the interior truth of the act or to the dignity of the communion of persons. The truth is not reciprocally expressed. In contraceptive intercourse, the truths of self-mastery, of the reciprocal gift, and of the reciprocal acceptance of self are lacking.

This violates the interior structure of the sexual act and constitutes the essential evil of the contraceptive act.

To understand this teaching, we must reflect on the concupiscence of the flesh.   *August 22, 1984*

120. HUMAN FERTILITY –
PART OF GOD'S BENEVOLENT PLAN

Need for Self-Mastery

The encyclical fully approves the natural regulation of fertility and responsible parenthood as long as artificial contraception is not used. For responsible parenthood, the couple must recognize the blessings of family life, and they must acquire complete mastery over themselves and their emotions.

Discipline of Periodic Continence

To control these natural drives, self-denial is needed. Only self-mastery will insure that their expression of love conforms to right order. The self-discipline of periodic continence doesn't hinder marital love but gives it a more human character.

Self-discipline, although demanding perseverance, enables the couple to develop their full personalities enriched by spiritual blessings (21). The encyclical shows the great benefits of periodic continence for the whole family, demanding from the spouses a definite family and procreative attitude (21).

Family Life

The 1980 Synod of Bishops "On the Role of the Christian Family" considered these questions. Later, the comprehensive Familiaris Consortium (The Apostolic Exhortation) treated these issues. Really, the theology of the body is rooted in a theology of the family and in a correct vision of the true values of family life.

A Fruit of the Spirit

When the Pope says that self-mastery in conjugal chastity lies in periodic continence (21), his doctrine on chastity is understood as a life in the Spirit (Gal. 5:25). Only periodic continence, the fruit of the Spirit, is the basis for a morally responsible parenthood.

Even though the "periodicity" of continence is applied to the natural biological rhythms, the continence itself is not biological. It demands strong ethical motivation. "To experience the gift of married love while respecting the laws of conception" acknowledges the design of the Creator (13). Pope John XXIII (Mater et Magister) wrote, "Human life is sacred. From its very beginning it directly involves the creative action of God"

Using Gods Benevolent Plan

Pope Paul VI said that the reasons for practicing periodic continence require "reasonable grounds for spacing births". These are based upon "the physical or psychological conditions of husband or wife, or from external circumstances" (16).

A spouse who uses periodic continence in the context of a morally upright regulation of fertility certainly lives by the Spirit of God (Gal. 5:25). This is called the "natural regulation". It is in conformity with the natural law, understood by reason and undertaken in fidelity to the Creator. Spouses must study this biological regularity because, as an expression of the order of nature, it is a part of God's benevolent plan.   *August 28, 1984*

121. PAYING ATTENTION TO THE ETHICAL DIMENSION

A Prophetic Call

The Book of Malachi reads: "The Lord was witness to the covenant between you and the wife of your youth. ... What does He desire? Godly offspring. So take heed to yourselves and let none be faithless to the wife of his youth." (2:14-15).

Discovering God's Design

The Pope calls the method "natural" because it corresponds to the truth and the dignity which belong to man as a free rational being. By his reason, man can discover the biological rhythm of nature. By his will, he can conform his actions to God's design inscribed in human fecundity.

These "natural rhythms contained in the generative process" are objective truths. A person's body speaks both externally, (by masculinity and femininity) and by the internal structures, (bodily and emotional reactions). These truths are part of the dialogue of the spouses in the communion of their bodies.

The efforts for precise knowledge of these rhythms are important because these rhythms are not just a biological language. They can be used by the husband and wife to express themselves sexually. Responsible parenthood (acting in truth) demands the continued effort and self-denial to respect the rhythm of nature (21). This morally correct regulation of fertility is based upon respect for God's design.

Abuses of Infertile Periods

Couples abuse the infertile periods when they lower the number of births below the morally correct level. This level is not just established by considering the good of the family and the health of the couple. The good of the Church, of society and of all mankind must be taken into account..

According to Pope Paul VI, responsible parenthood is not exclusively directed to limiting births. Its full meaning includes a willingness to accept a larger family and a "deeper relationship with the objective moral order"

Contrast With Modern Thought

Because Pope Paul VI stresses the virtue of temperance and the correct method of limiting births, his encyclical diverges widely from contemporary thought. This common viewpoint separates the ethical dimension from the functional, utilitarian approach. Modern thought sees no difference between the natural method and artificial contraception.

This ethical dimension cannot be set aside. Attention must be given to self-mastery and continence, because these alone can lead to the real truth about man. A true theology of the body shows that the natural method alone is morally correct.

Many Good Results

The effects are many. Pope Paul VI says that this self-discipline brings tranquility and peace, repels excessive self-love, and awakens a consciousness of responsibilities. It gives the parents a more effective influence over their children, who are taught a right sense of values and a better use of their mental and physical powers (21). This lawful ordering of births is not just a specific mode of behavior but an attitude based on moral maturity.

September 5, 1984

122. FINDING SPIRITUALITY IN THE CHURCH'S TRADITIONS

A Door to Christian Spirituality

Although the Church gives laws, she also opens channels of grace and makes us children of God. The vocation of Christian husbands and wives is rooted in Baptism and is explicitly confirmed in Matrimony. In this sacrament they are consecrated to make visible the holiness and the joy of their inseparable union and their cooperation with God (25).

By showing the moral evil of the contraceptive act and the framework of responsible parenthood, Pope Paul provides married couples with an opportunity for the Christian spirituality which is contained in the Church's traditions. The theology of the body contains the essential aspects for this true conjugal spirituality.

Need For Spirituality

Responsible parenthood must not be reduced to merely following biological rhythms, (a false interpretation of Pope Paul's teaching). Full responsible parenthood is an important element of conjugal spirituality. The spouses must "realize to the full their vocation" (HV 25) and receive from the sacrament the needed "strengthening powers" (25).

Pope Paul does not pass "over in silence the difficulties, at times very great" for "the gate is narrow that leads to life" (Mt.7:14). There is need "to live sober, upright and godly lives in this world" (Ti. 2:12) because "the form of this world is passing away" (1Cor. 7:31) (25).

Christian realism teaches an urgency. The spouses must acquire the powers that come from a full spirituality of marriage.

Need for Sacraments

The couples must be guided through the difficult times by an awareness of heavenly life. In this way, they can take up the burden appointed to them, and God's love will be poured out into our hearts (Rom.5:5) (25). Because the Holy Spirit Himself plants this essential power of love, the couple must draw grace from the Eucharist and pardon from the Sacrament of Penance. These are the infallible and indispensable means to form marital and family spirituality. *October 3, 1984*

123. LOVE RESOLVES THE CONTRADICTION

Love Leads to Truth

Love is a capacity given to man to participate in God's mystery of creation and redemption. Love always rejoices, because God rejoiced when He saw that everything "was very good". (Gen.1:31)

While the power of concupiscence falsifies the language of the body, love always strengthens the truth of this language.

Love brings about a conjugal dialogue according to full truth, and orients the spouses toward the fullness of good. Love is a moral power which safeguards the inseparable connection between the two meanings of union and procreation. Love protects both the value of the personal union and the value of responsible parenthood.

Deepening the Traditional Teaching

Traditional language describes love as a higher power which coordinates the actions of the spouses in their married life. In marriage, God gives the spouses this higher power and a unique consecration. Their love and consecration involve an orientation to the true purpose of marriage and the moral order.

The Council and Pope Paul affirm and deepen the traditional teaching when they state that love confers value upon the conjugal acts in accord with its two purposes, unitive and procreative.

No Contradiction

Love protects the value of a true communion of persons and responsible parenthood, correctly uniting these two meanings of the conjugal act. The power of love excludes, in theory and in practice, the contradiction which is sometimes claimed to exist in the Church's teaching. There is no contradiction in the teaching, even though there is difficulty in obeying the teaching. The encyclical mentions this in various passages.

The Real Difficulty and Solution

The difficulty arises because this power of love is implanted in persons who are burdened by concupiscence (1Jn.2:16), especially the concupiscence of the flesh which distorts the truth of the body. In historical man, love can realize the truth only by overcoming concupiscence.

Love requires chastity, the mastery over self through continence, especially periodic continence. Paul alludes to this in Ephesians, "defer to one another out of reverence for Christ" (5:21). The encyclical, therefore, is a development of this biblical truth.   *October 10, 1984*

124. ENRICHING MARRIED LIFE BY OVERCOMING CONCUPISCENCE

The Power to Dominate and Direct

Continence is the capacity to dominate, control and direct drives of a sexual character (called concupiscence of the flesh). Continence shapes the consequences of the sexual drive within the subjectivity of the person. When continence is a constant disposition of the will, it is called a virtue.

Continence Versus Concupiscence

Concupiscence of the flesh (and the sexual desires which accompany it) result in specific impulses in the sphere of bodily reactions and emotional excitements of the sensual impulse. To conquer these, the person must be committed to a progressive self-control of will and feelings. This "education in self-mastery" presupposes a clear perception and a firm conviction of true values.

If the person's will is rightly disposed, the virtue of continence will result. This self-mastery (continence) is necessary so that the couple can "defer to one another" (a mutual concern that the language of their bodies is true). This deference is "out of reverence for Christ" (Gal. 5:21) and is based upon the fear of God (piety), a gift of the Holy Spirit.

Although continence, especially periodic continence, controls the concupiscence of the flesh, it is not complete by itself. It must be connected with prudence, justice, fortitude and especially, charity.

Gaining More Mature Values

By resisting concupiscence, continence leads to more mature values in the spousal relationship and to the authentic freedom needed for mutual self-giving. Concupiscence (which always seeks sensual satisfaction) can make the spouses blind and insensitive to the deeper values which constitute true love.

By continence and conjugal chastity, spouses can "defer to one another" and foster the needed interior independence which makes them sensitive to the more profound values of marriage.

Enriching Sexual Expression

At first, conjugal chastity focuses on resisting the concupiscence of the flesh. Later, it reveals the person's capacity to express meanings of the body's language in ways which were hidden by concupiscence. These deeper meanings purify and simplify the marital dialogue. This sexual asceticism does not impoverish but enriches affective manifestations, making them spiritually more intense.

Difficulties Arising From Concupiscence

In objecting to the Church's teaching, some claim that there is a contradiction between the unitive meaning and the procreative meaning. Therefore, it must be licit to separate the two. Actually no contradiction exists between these two meanings. In a person given over to concupiscence, there is difficulty in practicing this virtue because concupiscence does not bring about a true ordering of the conjugal life. Only an interior, virtuous commitment, in which the couple are strengthened and consecrated, can accomplish conjugal truth (25).

Conjugal chastity creates harmony between responsible parenthood and personal communion. When the spouses mature spiritually, the conjugal act acquires its true dignity of being potentially procreative. At the same time, their affective manifestations express a rich subjective personal communion.

Other Manifestations of Affection

The encyclical says that conjugal union is a "manifestation of affection" (16), which is also potentially procreative. Certainly, the couple can licitly manifest their affections in ways that express their personal union but are not directly procreative. Conjugal chastity protects the procreative meaning of the conjugal act and reveals to the couple many other ways in which they can express personal union.

Chastity does no harm to the personal union. When the couple abstains from the conjugal act, they can use other manifestations of love. These prepare the way for those days when a morally right conjugal act can take place.   *October 24, 1984*

125. CONTINENCE – MAINTAINING A BALANCE BETWEEN EXCITEMENT AND EMOTION

Inner Tensions

Many believe that continence causes inner tensions. In reality, continence is the only way for the person to be free from such tensions. Continence is the spiritual effort needed to express the "language of the body" in the authentic richness of affective manifestations.

Urgent Questions

The most urgent questions are, "Is this effort possible?" and "Is this moral law feasible?" The Church believes in the correctness of this moral principal because responsible parenthood corresponds with the dignity of the persons and of the conjugal act. Truly responsible parenthood is linked to the spirituality of marriage.

Pope Paul VI wrote that the focus must be on the person who makes the decision and not upon the means which depersonalize. This question concerns the truly authentic meaning of human progress.

Not A Biological Question

"Is this effort possible?" The Pope does not reduce the answer to the biological dimension of fertility but goes to that personal "I" of the man and woman.

The Council had already demanded a deeper understanding of human reactions and emotions in the mutual influence of the masculine and the feminine. This question belongs to psychology more than to biology. The answer must include periodic continence, and a true idea of responsible parenthood. Obviously, this profoundly personalistic question cannot be resolved at a biological level.

Excitement and Emotions

Human psychology shows clearly that reactions (excitement and emotions), are part of the mutual influence of masculinity-femininity. However, excitement and emotions are also quite distinguished from each other. Excitement is corporeal and sensual, while emotions see the other person in his/her integrity. Emotions are caused by the other person in his/her masculinity or femininity.

We must not focus on the negative role of continence (such as the ability to abstain or as a mastery over various sexual reactions). Continence has a positive role of correctly directing sexual reactions, both in their content and in their quality.

Maintaining a Balance

Excitement and emotion, although distinct, often do appear as two elements of a single experience. Sometime one predominates and, at other times, the two are maintained in a balance.

Because continence directs excitement and emotion, its essential task is to maintain this balance. In this way, the couple can mutually express their intimate union in which they implicitly accept procreation. Often excitement and emotion can jeopardize the mutual reciprocity of the gift.

Diverse Goals

Because excitement is expressed in sensual pleasure, its goal is toward the conjugal act which includes procreation. Emotion, caused by the masculinity/ femininity, can limit itself to other manifestations of affection which express the spousal meaning without including the procreative meaning. Obviously, moral conclusions come from these observations.   *October 31, 1984*

126. CONTINENCE DIRECTS THE SENSUAL AND EMOTIONAL REACTIONS

The Real Goals

Continence certainly controls bodily reactions. However, the great classical thinkers, both non-Christian and Christian (St. Thomas Aquinas), see continence as the person's capacity to control and to guide man's sensual and emotional responses. The question here is the power of continence to direct excitement toward its correct development and to guide emotion toward its deepest and purest character.

Excitement and Emotions

The conjugal act, which results from excitement, must involve the deepest emotions of the person. It should also involve an intensification of the other person's emotions. "Defer to one another out of reverence for Christ." (Eph.5:21) seeks this mutual intensification.

The distinction between excitement and emotion shows the subjective richness of the human "I", which excludes any reduction to the merely biological level. The couple needs continence to correctly direct excitement and emotion. Continence can maintain the interior balance between excitement and emotion and between the personal communion and procreation.

Must Be Part of A Spirituality

Humanae Vitae calls the rhythmic character of human fertility both "a periodicalness", and "a providential index for responsible parenthood". Therefore, the regulation of births is a profoundly personalistic question and cannot be answered on the biological level. Responsible parenthood is a proof of a mature conjugal love. It is not just an "ethical answer" but is really a "plan for conjugal spirituality."

Discovering the "Naturalness"

Practicing periodic continence as part of marital spirituality is the secret in discovering the "naturalness" of the method (which must always be at the level of the person). The mere knowledge of the rhythms of fertility does not provide the needed interior freedom. This freedom depends on "inner spiritual maturity" and gives the person a capacity to direct the sensual and emotional reactions to a free giving of self.

The human body, masculine and feminine, is ordered to the communion of persons. This "meaning of the body" has been distorted by concupiscence of the flesh. Continence reveals anew the body's pure "spousal meaning" and develops the personal communion. These gifts cannot be formed at the level of concupiscence. *November 7, 1984*

127. CONJUGAL CHASTITY - UNDERSTOOD AND LIVED ONLY IN THE SPIRIT'S POWER

Proper Developing of Affective Manifestations

In the sacrament of matrimony, the couple receives the Holy Spirit and a special consecration. Love, when coupled with a conjugal chastity, brings about the interior ordering of the spouses' life.

Chastity permits a proper development of the manifestations of affection. This development is called "life by the Spirit" (Gal.5:25). Although Paul was conscious of the immanent energies of the human spirit, he primarily meant the sanctifying power of the Holy Spirit. Chastity is a virtue given by the Holy Spirit which brings about the proper development of the spouses' manifestations of affection. This correct ordering of married life is really a gift of the Holy Spirit with which the couple needs to cooperate.

Cooperating With the Spirit

The couple must be committed to acquiring those virtues (love, chastity, and continency) which give a sensitivity to the Spirit. The couple cannot bring their bodily union to the level of persons except through the Holy Spirit. "It is the Spirit that gives life; the flesh is useless." (Jn.6:3)

The couple must accept the essential truths of conjugal spirituality (which are contained in the beginning biblical teaching) and they must be open to the Spirit. The encyclical speaks of their being open to the Spirit by unremitting prayer, the reception of Eucharist and recourse to the Sacrament of Penance (25).

The Spirit Bestows Respect

By respecting the sacred, the couple will have a particular sensitivity for the mystery of creation and of redemption. Through the Spirit, they can receive a respect for the two meanings of the conjugal act. They can enjoy a profound reverence for both the personal dignity of the spouse and for the new life which can be conceived. In this way, the spouses respect God's creation, and have a salvific fear of violating or degrading whatever bears the sign of the mystery of creation and redemption. "Defer to one another out of reverence for Christ" speaks of this Godly fear.

Effects of This Reverence

In a negative sense, this reverence is evident in resisting concupiscence. Positively, this reverence produces a sensitivity and veneration for the sacred value of the two meanings of the conjugal act (the interior truth of the language of the body). This profound reverence enables the seeming contradiction (that Church teaching would destroy human love) to disappear and the difficulties from concupiscence to be overcome.

The Spirit Gives Authentic Maturity
Respect for God's gifts reconciles human dignity with the natural fertility cycles, (the biological dimension of the body). Because of the Spirit, the biological and conjugal union in the flesh can find a humanly mature form. The upright regulation of fertility linked to responsible parenthood forms part of marital spirituality. Only by living "in the Spirit" can it become authentic.

November 14, 1984

128. RESPECT NEEDED FOR PERSONAL COMMUNION

Piety Respects God's Actions
Piety (the Spirit's gift) respects God's actions and helps to clarify the conjugal act (in which the spousal meaning and the procreative meaning are linked). Only by piety, can the couple understand the conjugal act's singular significance and the serious responsibility of possible parenthood.

When piety is lacking, a contraceptive practice and mentality emerges which does tremendous harm. In contrast, when piety and conjugal chastity form the couple's spirituality, they protect the particular dignity of the act and safeguard the act's procreative potential.

By responsible parenthood, the spouses conform their knowledge and will to the truth of the conjugal act. They manifest their affection in a mature readiness for parenthood, considering all of the circumstances, including the biological ones.

The Power of Respect
Respect for God's work (piety) safeguards the conjugal act from being diminished, deprived of meaning, or becoming merely a habit. By piety, the conjugal act has its full personal content and expresses veneration for the Creator. Also, the spouses' mutual freedom is enlarged because they express the full spousal meaning of their act. While piety strengthens freedom, concupiscence has the opposite effect. It constricts inner freedom because the other person is seen as an object of pleasure.

Daily Manifestations

The spouses must have a profound appreciation of the personal dignity of the masculine "I" and the feminine "I". They must respect God's creation so that their affectionate manifestations can acquire a spousal meaning. Although the conjugal act is used only at times, affection should be manifested every day by various acts flowing from selfless emotion.

Respect for God's work has enormous significance in these daily manifestations in which there is deep satisfaction and disinterested attention to the visible and invisible beauty of the masculine/feminine.

Physical Manifestations

This personal satisfaction and admiration show both the visible and the invisible beauty of what God has made male and female. From this awareness, there come physical manifestations of affection which safeguard the couples' inner freedom and help them to remain faithful to their union. These manifestations promote a deep-rooted peace (the interior echo of chastity).

A Suitable Climate

Piety demands a profound attention to the other person and creates a climate suitable for personal communion in which responsible procreation can mature. Conjugal spirituality must create this human and supernatural climate. Although this spirituality considers the biological order, it really is formed by chastity and piety. True marital harmony demands the interior truth of both love and procreation.   *November 21, 1984*

129. A SUMMARY OF THE TEACHING SERIES

The title for these four years of teachings is "Human love in the Divine Plan" or, more precisely, "The Redemption of the Body and the Sacramentality of Marriage"

Initial Teachings and Ephesians

The initial teachings were based on three sayings of Jesus. First, Jesus used the phrase "in the beginning" when discussing divorce with the Pharisees (Mt.19:8 and Mk.10: 6-9). Second, in His Sermon on the Mount, He described concupiscence as "adultery committed in the heart" (Mt.5:28). Third, He referred to the resurrection of the body in the other world. (Mt.22:30; Mk.12:25 and Lk.20:35).

After those initial teachings, we focused on Ephesians 5:21-33 which included the words of Genesis, "A man leaves his mother and father and clings to his wife, and the two of them become one body." (2:24)

A "Working Term"

The phrase "Theology of the Body" was used throughout. It was a "working term" which correctly expressed the theme, "The Redemption of the Body and the Sacramentality of Marriage." Obviously, a full "Theology of the Body" goes far beyond these reflections and includes other problems, such as suffering and death.

These reflections on the body's redemption and the sacramentality of marriage were based on the revelation in Genesis, that "the two of them became one body", a foundation confirmed by Christ who refers to "the beginning".

Marriage as a Sacrament

These reflections on marriage as a sacrament had two dimensions, that of grace and of sign. In both dimensions (and in analyzing Humanae Vitae), we went back to the key words of Christ.

Because the encyclical is related to the sacramentality of marriage and to the theology of the body, we needed to reflect on the redemption of the body and the sacramentality of marriage to respond to the modern questions concerning conjugal and family morality. The widespread reaction caused by the encyclical shows the importance and difficulty of these questions.

Development of Theology

"The Role of the Christian Family" (1980 Synod of Bishops) asks theologians to elaborate the personalistic aspects of

Humanae Vitae and requests that the questions and answers focus on the biblical and personalistic aspects.

This request points out the trend in the development of the theology of the body and how this theology can be completed. By using the biblical aspects, the Church places its teaching on the foundation of revelation, the true basis of every true theological development.

Church doctrine must always be open to questions posed by man. There has been an intense development of human ethics which closely interconnects with these theological questions faced by Humanae Vitae.

The Modern Trend

Our analysis has been based on the truth about the progress of man. Unfortunately, there is a tendency in Western culture (both hidden and explicit) to measure progress in terms of material good and not in terms of personal growth.

Pope Paul VI made a determined appeal to counteract this trend and to measure progress on the basis of the person, (of what is good for man as man). The encyclical shows that true human development is measured by ethics not by technology.

Conclusions Based on Beginning Teachings

This final catechesis focused on Humanae Vitae and treated questions which are very important to the modern world. These questions permeate all our previous reflections and they were not artificially added on. Our final conclusions are really contained in the beginning reflections.

The Task Completed

These reflections began in preparation for the 1980 Bishop's Synod and concluded after the publication of their statement "The Role of the Christian Family". Formulating answers to the questions raised by the encyclical demanded a clear analysis of the biblical–theological sphere. This is the basis for the redemption of the body and the sacramentality of marriage. Here, we find answers to both the perennial questions and to the difficult questions of modern man. *November 28, 1984*